"I've had the opportunity to worl
nonprofit world. I've found his ac
to be instructive. I highly recommenu uus vvvn. nuuiuonany, as chair
of the Museum of the Bible, we are implementing many of these cutting-
edge fundraising thoughts."

Steve Green | President, Hobby Lobby, Inc.

"*Charity Shock* is the new field guide for effective fundraising. Bill High
and Ray Gary offer nonprofit leaders an eyes-wide-open survey of the
changing landscape. They cover the new frontier, threatening terrain,
alternative routes, and how to master the tools sure to unlock generous
giving. This book equips you well with exactly what you need to deeply
engage all generations in your ministry and mission."

Tami Heim | President & CEO, Christian Leadership Alliance

"Occasionally in your life you come across that guy. The one that
challenges you through his creativity and intellect to think differently
about fundraising and family generosity. Bill High is that guy. I am
honored to have worked with him in a variety of different capacities
over the past twenty years. When it comes to creative giving strategy
and major donor engagement, he is the go-to guy. I can only give my
highest recommendation and endorsement of the man and his writing."

Tim Smith | Former Chief Development Officer, Museum of the
Bible; and current President, Timothy Smith & Associates

"Is your ministry skating to where the 'puck' of donor dollars used
to be? If so, Bill High has written a masterpiece of must-read wise
counsel for you! After painting a compelling picture of the changing
landscape in ministry fundraising, Bill helps you transition away from
the wave of whatever former successes you've had in this area, and
toward the emerging opportunities before you now with older donors,
new technologies, giving beyond cash, and much more."

Mike Buwalda | Founder of Money for Ministry, planned giving services,
and host of the Christian Leadership Alliance "Encore" webcast series

CHARITY

SHOCK

CHARITY SHOCK

Bill High with Ray Gary

Foreword by Dan Busby, President, ECFA

Charity Shock.

Cover and interior design by Stephanie Ibarra.

DEDICATION

To all those who labor diligently in
ministry for the greater good: your sacrificial
service is to be commended. May this book
provide greater fuel for your mission.

CONTENTS

FOREWORD

As the president of the Evangelical Council for Financial Accountability (ECFA), I have the opportunity to work with many nonprofit organizations and churches around the country. Part of our aim is to make the nonprofit world better by providing and enforcing uniform standards. That desire to make the nonprofit world better is one of the reasons why I'm writing this foreword.

Bill High and Ray Gary have written a masterful and necessary work for the nonprofit world. As I read the manuscript and consider the trends they've outlined, I can't help but think of my nightly weather forecast. It's great to be able to turn on the television, the radio, or my computer and look at predictions for what the weather will hold.

On the other hand, when I think about those weather forecasts, it makes me realize that we have no weatherman for the nonprofit world. But things change, conditions change, and someone needs to forecast how those changes will affect the nonprofit world.

That's what *Charity Shock* is about—providing a forecast to the nonprofit world. And I believe that "shock" really should be in the title. Things are changing. Some of that change is great. Some of it will bring real opportunity. Some of it will not. But I'm afraid that many in the nonprofit sector are not ready or even aware of that change.

Even in the work of the ECFA, I'm surprised by how many organizations are not aware of rule changes that negatively impact their operations. So many times those organizations get caught in the same patterns of doing work the same old way.

Change is in the wind. I'm hoping that the whole of the nonprofit world will read this book and adjust to those changing winds. Those adjustments will help determine the strong future of service nonprofit organizations bring to our world.

Dan Busby
President
Evangelical Council for
Financial Accountability

PREFACE

Have you felt the tremors? Over the past decade, the ground we stand on as fundraisers has shifted dramatically.

After the economic crash of 2008, many news articles came out lamenting how long it would take the fundraising world to "get back to normal." At The Signatry, we were quick to warn the non-profits we worked with that we were facing a new normal. Fundraising methods that had worked in the past wouldn't work much longer. However, most organizations failed to adjust to the fundamental shifts in the fundraising world. Not that they blatantly ignored them; it's just that few realized what was happening.

In *The Age Curve*, market analyst Kenneth Gronbach illustrates the importance of recognizing and adjusting to the changing times. Before 1986, American Honda Motorcycle thrived as Gronbach's premier advertising account. Honda had grown using a fairly simple model: Ship bikes from the warehouse to the dealers, run ads, and make sales. But in 1986, two months after shipping, nothing happened. No sales.

In fact, sales continued to drop for the *next six years*. By 1992, most Honda dealerships were ready to close. What had gone wrong?

It took Gronbach several years to figure out what was really a simple answer: The market demographics had shifted and no one noticed. Before 1986, the majority of motorcycle sales came from the Boomer generation. But by 1986, most Boomers had reached age twenty-seven. At age twenty-seven they were married and had their first child. The baby won, and the motorcycle got the boot.

Fast-forward to the present day, and we find the fundraising world in a similar industry-altering shift. While giving has come back, to a degree, from the depths of the 2008 recession, the rebound has not by any means been a "return to normal." But as with American Honda Motorcycle, few nonprofits have recognized this shift, and they're starting to pay dearly for it.

That's why we are writing this book. We live in the middle of a revolution, and the battle tactics have changed. Old methods of fundraising simply don't work anymore, or they yield smaller results. Instead of trying harder or changing staff, it's time to look outside our organizations and ask what's changed in the world around us.

The changes are drastic. Competition has risen as nonprofits have multiplied, each one clamoring for their share of funds. At the same time, the pool of donors and the dollars they give has remained relatively unchanged. Good sense urges us to gather major gifts from an aging donor audience and at the same time cultivate a younger generation of givers—a task requiring two different messages and two different approaches. Meanwhile, a brand-new tactic is emerging in capturing gifts other than cash, such as stock and real estate. The list of changes could go on and on.

These are urgent times, as new generations replace the older giving generations—new generations that are smaller, younger, and squeezed for resources because of high taxes, inflation, and runaway government spending. The good news, however, is that we are also undergoing the largest transfer of wealth in human history, perhaps as much as $40 trillion. That money will go either to heirs, to an increasingly voracious government, or to nonprofits. The window of great and unprecedented opportunity is wide open today. Forward-thinking organizations will climb through it. Others will not.

Will your organization be one that captures a share of those dollars to accomplish your vision? You are about to find out!

Bill High
Kansas City

Ray Gary
Dallas

INTRODUCTION

The Changed Landscape of Fundraising

"When you can't change the direction of
the wind—adjust your sails."

H. JACKSON BROWN, JR.

Everyone who knows hockey knows Wayne Gretzky. "The Great One," as he came to be called, dominated the National Hockey League (NHL) for two decades. People said he had a "sixth sense" or "eyes in the back of his head" when it came to hockey. Many of his feats, including most goals scored, still stand as NHL records. He is the leading scorer in NHL history, has completed the most assists, and still holds sixty NHL records. He is the most successful hockey player of all time.

Ask Gretzky the reason for his success, and he'll respond simply yet profoundly, "I skate to where the puck is going to be, not where it has been."[1]

While onlookers credited his success to an intuitive ability to play hockey, Gretzky knew there was more involved than simple intuition. From age three to seventeen, his father drilled him on how to anticipate where the puck would be. In *Gretzky: An Autobiography*, Gretzky recounts how his dad would tell him, "This is how everybody else does it." He would shoot the puck into the corner of the rink, and then chase after it as it bounced off the wall and across the ice. Next his dad would say, "And this is how a smart player does it." He would then hit the puck to the corner of the rink just as before, but this time instead of chasing after it, he would cut across the rink to be ready to meet the puck as it came to him. From this exercise, Gretzky learned to skate to where the puck was going, not where it had been.[2]

What do Wayne Gretzky and hockey have to do with fundraising? The same strategy that propelled Gretzky to success will help your nonprofit. Too many ministries and nonprofit organizations are waking up to find they have been skating to where the puck, or their donors, *used to be*. Nonprofit organizations spend their time chasing after where their donors were before, and then they wonder why their fundraising methods don't work. They spend more money on development programs, hire new directors, fire directors who don't produce, and repeat the cycle—all the while hoping to get different results. And when their results remain the same or become worse, they wonder why. Doing the same actions and expecting different results? I think that's what they call insanity.

Most nonprofit organizations don't realize that the giving landscape has changed at all, let alone *why* it has changed. Blind to these changes, they don't take steps toward improvement until it's too late and their organization teeters on the brink of death. They have no idea where the puck is headed or how to get there.

Like Gretzky, it's time nonprofits worked smarter, not harder. As a nonprofit, you need to learn to anticipate where donors are headed and how to meet them there. This book will help you do that. You'll learn where they're going and how to anticipate their changes. But before we can understand how to change, we must understand where nonprofits currently stand.

The Game Changers

A popular business book in the late 1990s asked the question, *Who Moved My Cheese?* This book's message was that businesses must adjust to change. It illustrated this point by humorously chronicling two men and two mice who lived in a maze and daily chased after cheese. Once they found a cheese stash, both pairs got into a routine of eating from that stash every day. When the cheese was moved, the mice quickly started exploring the maze to find the new cheese. Meanwhile the two men, instead of moving on, stayed and complained about the fact that their cheese was missing. They were slow to move out into the maze in search of new cheese. The moral of the story was that the more quickly we embrace change, the more quickly we'll benefit from that change.

As with *Who Moved My Cheese?* an equally pressing question for nonprofits today is "Who moved my dollars?" Nonprofits are using the same methods they've used for decades, but they've stopped receiving the same results. Old methods aren't as effective as they used to be. Instead of blindly pressing on and refusing to acknowledge that the fundraising landscape isn't what it used to be, they need to stop and look at what's changed. Then they need to figure out how to adjust their methods to meet those changes head-on.

Looking for a single cause of dwindling donations is like investing in the stock market using a single metric. It can't be done. Just like a host of factors play on the stock market to influence its ebb and flow, many factors work together in the nonprofit field to change both the playing field and the rules of the game. Before we elaborate on the changes that are affecting nonprofits, let's first take a look at the present situation. After all, in order to know where donors are headed, we need to know where they are right now.

Consider the following information:

1.   Giving as a percentage of income still remains stuck at 2 percent. In other words, people aren't giving any more of their income than in the past. Whether we're in an economic crash or in a time of affluence, giving, on average, has remained at this percent.

9

2. The number of nonprofits is increasing, which means there are more organizations fishing in the same pond. There's more competition for the same number of dollars.

3. Since the bulk of giving still comes from the War Generations and Boomers, the number of givers is decreasing. As these generations grow older, there are fewer people in the succeeding generations, and statistics show that they give less. (We'll expound more on the generations in Chapter 1.)

4. While there is an immediate opportunity to obtain major and planned gifts, some factors remain unknown, such as economics, tax policies, and the Millennials' development as a giving generation.

In light of all these changes—static giving, more nonprofits, fewer givers, and unknown factors—nonprofits face more struggles than ever. They still need funding just as much as before, but it's becoming increasingly difficult to find that funding. Let's take a deeper look into each of the struggles.

More Demand, Less Supply

Giving is growing, but not as fast as the demand for gifts. According to the Giving USA Foundation, in 2016, overall charitable contributions rose to the highest amount seen in sixty years. Individuals and institutions gave $390 billion, a 3 percent increase from the previous year. However, this positive report misrepresents the gifts that religious organizations have received, because these gifts have dropped over the past thirty years by 21 percent. Moreover, giving as a percentage of income has remained at 2 percent for essentially forty years.[3] While the nonprofit industry has done much to promote the idea of generosity, giving as a percentage of income has not increased. And finally, population growth has remained flat. We simply are not adding as many new givers or dollars to the giving pool.

Meanwhile, more nonprofits are competing for their share. The National Center for Charitable Statistics estimates that as of 2012 there were 2.3 million nonprofit organizations in America, which would mean roughly one nonprofit for every 140 citizens.[4]

With this growing number of nonprofits, there is more demand than ever for charitable gifts, but the supply has not risen to meet the need.

More Noise, More Methods

With the rising number of nonprofits comes an increased variety of fundraising methods. In order to understand the current sphere of fundraising, let's take a brief tour of the history of charitable giving, beginning with religious giving. First there was the offering plate. Churches would pass the plate down rows of pews and ask people to plunk in their dollars and coins. Then mission agencies perfected the art of raising support. Missionaries would have dinner in people's homes and invite them to informative lectures where the missionaries would show slides of distant lands and then share about the need for their work. At the end of these dinners or slideshows, they would invite donors to become lifelong supporters of their mission work and commit to regular giving. Then charity went mainstream. Direct mail brought all forms of requests—varied envelope sizes, catchy subject lines, anecdotal stories, and solemn pleas. Nonprofits grew increasingly creative in ways to gather money. Events, auctions, golf tournaments, celebrity dinners, and getaway weekends have all had their day as effective fundraisers.

Within the last few decades, the rise of technology has added an entirely new component to fundraising. Email campaigns, online giving techniques, payment systems, and mobile giving have revolutionized the ways that nonprofits can gather donations. Through social media, crowdfunding has exploded, meaning that any average Joe can become a fundraiser without having to go through all the paperwork of starting a nonprofit. At every turn, people are asking donors to give in new ways.

Today, all of these methods have piled up on top of each other to the point where most of these requests are ignored, thrown away, or deleted. As one of our donor friends said, "It's just too confusing." As a survival strategy, donors have learned to tune out constant appeals for money. In a world inundated with requests, you've got to learn to cut through the noise and make sure your nonprofit's message is heard above the rest.

Generational Change

In addition to a dwindling supply of gifts and greater competition, nonprofits are also facing the challenge of the changing preferences of each succeeding generation. We'll discuss demographic trends at length in the next chapter, but the important point to understand now is that there are multiple generations of givers, each with different giving capacities, values, and expectations: the War Generations, the Baby Boomers, Generation X, and the Millennials.

Suppose you send exactly the same letter to a list of ten thousand people who are a mix of all generations. You are likely to get a vastly different response from each generation. Fundraisers act as if one size fits all, but that's not the case anymore. One size does not fit all. Each age group's preferences determine how likely they are to respond to your appeal for donations. However, many nonprofits are not catering their appeals to the different generations. In order to stay on top of their game, they need to learn to be in tune with each generation's needs.

Uncertain Politics, Uncertain Economy

In light of an uncertain economy, nonprofits can feel like they're standing on shaky ground. The crash of 2008 was more than an event. It unlocked a latent discussion, prompting Americans to rethink government responsibility, regulation, and debt. The debt questions have led to revenue questions. How will our country fund our debt, growth, and infrastructure needs?

For the first time, many in Congress and even the White House feel the freedom to question the viability of the charitable income tax deduction. What many have viewed as sacred—giving to charity—may now become a revenue source for the federal government.

Likewise, the overall economy and state of the stock market produced at times a prevailing insecurity, if not fear, in the US public. Typically, charitable giving rises as people's confidence in the economy rises, and giving dips down as people's confidence dips. The 2008 crash revealed troubling cracks in our foundation that have caused many to hold onto their pennies for the perceived upcoming rainy days. In the upcoming chapters, we'll discuss how nonprofits must respond to an uncertain government and economy, and how their response will influence the future of nonprofits.

Revolutionary Change, Revolutionary Opportunity

When I worked as a lawyer, we had a lawsuit involving a large warehouse in Fort Scott, Kansas. Everything that could possibly go wrong had gone wrong with that building. The building wasn't square, so the floors weren't flat. The floors weren't flat, so they cracked. The cracked floors wore out the forklifts' wheels. And on and on and on. There was no end to the problems this building had.

In the end, it came down to carelessness by everyone involved. The builders hadn't noticed the building wasn't square. The concrete mixer that laid the floors had used an old truck that couldn't get a good mix. Even the architect had allowed the building to be designed for the wrong wind load. (It gets pretty windy out in the Kansas prairie.)

Each builder was so entrenched in their day-to-day work that they couldn't see the errors staring them in the face. But at the end of the lawsuit, the builders still had to pay for their mistakes.

In the nonprofit world, it's easy to do the same. Most people live in paragraphs and never understand the full story. My goal in writing this book is to lift nonprofit leaders up out of the paragraph— the daily grind of fundraising and running an organization—and to help you understand the full story going on around you.

Years ago, leaders used to focus solely on meeting the needs of those they were called to serve. Now they must also address multiple fundraising issues:

1. Providing planned giving solutions to an aging donor base.

2. Capturing a younger donor base while still reaching older donors.

3. Becoming technology integrators with endless options for fundraising: online giving, text giving, payment systems, contact-management systems, email campaigns, social media, etc.

4. Navigating government regulation related to tax rates, hiring practices and tax deductions.

5. Projecting their message loud enough to make sure it's heard above the many voices of competing nonprofits.

6. Proving their value both to increasingly selective donors

and to a government trying to replace charities with federal programs.

In the midst of these changes, many nonprofits are losing the game. They're falling behind in funding because they're still using the same playbook that was outdated a generation ago.

But there is good news.

With revolutionary change comes revolutionary opportunity. We are undergoing perhaps the most significant wealth transfer in the history of our world. An estimated $40 trillion dollars will pass from one generation to the next by 2050.[5]

As this wealth transfer occurs, significant dollars will be available for nonprofit organizations. Those dollars will go to the organizations that have learned to be the most skilled in anticipating donors' needs and meeting them. Through this book, you'll learn how to serve donors in new ways, tell compelling stories, make giving simple, and encourage noncash donations—to name a few.

Where is the puck headed in your nonprofit world? Let's skate there to meet it.

* * *

TREND ONE

How Generational Shifts Are Changing Fundraising

"The secret of change is to focus all of your energy, not
on fighting the old, but on building the new."

SOCRATES

For years, General Motors tried to stave off the death of its Oldsmobile brand. Born in 1897 and lasting over a century, Oldsmobile was a longstanding icon for the American dream. The brand became famous for its innovative cars. Throughout the twentieth century, the Oldsmobile was always the first in new technology. It was the first car to win a race against a locomotive, the first with front wheel drive, the first with turbo charge, and even the first with airbags. By 1985, their sales peaked at 1.2 million, making them the go-to brand for tech-savvy customers. But over the next five years, their sales nose-dived by 60 percent. In the late eighties and into the nineties, General Motors desperately tried to save the brand, even coining the phrase, "This is not your father's Oldsmobile" for a commercial and pulling in Ringo Starr—an icon from the last generation. Despite all their effort, however, sales continued to decline. Oldsmobile eked along for another decade until finally in 2004 General Motors pulled the plug.

What happened to this longstanding American icon? General Motors refused to adapt their car to the next generation, and so the Oldsmobile died off. They tried to ride the wave of former success indefinitely. Instead of adapting and creating new innovative cars for new generations, they did the opposite. They stopped being innovative and started modeling Oldsmobile to be like other car brands, such as Buicks and Chevys. Nothing set them apart. Although older generations still thought of Oldsmobile as a state-of-the-art car and associated it with the latest technology, newer generations didn't. Since General Motors failed to innovate, Oldsmobile faded into oblivion.

Like Oldsmobile, nonprofits must recognize the coming changes driven by generational influence. It's important to adjust to new generations and not just keep doing what worked for past generations. Even though a strategy worked in the past, this does not guarantee it will work in the future. Fundraisers must look at each generation with fresh eyes, and a nonprofit's tactics must be adjusted to the changing times. When we fail to adjust to a new generation, we will reap the consequences.

The Four Generations

I was sitting in Starbucks several years ago, reading an article on demographic trends and how they're affecting the financial world. The article covered investments, changes in the market, and how the age of our population was influencing the financial world. *The Wall Street Journal* was all over this stuff. The business world understands that changes in people equal changes in money. The nonprofit world doesn't. As CEO of a nonprofit, I knew that no one was relating these trends to the nonprofit sphere.

Yet the same changes that affect the financial world affect us nonprofits too. Donations come from the same bank accounts as consumer purchases. Our population is in the middle of some drastic changes. Although no one is talking about it, the changes are taking their toll on our fundraising.

Demographics matter. A population's size and makeup affect people's methods and motivations for giving. As fundraisers, we can't change the number of people in the world. We can't change what's happening. We can, however, look at the hard facts and then change our practices. We must study the generations at hand, since knowing how they behave yields important insights for the future. In this discussion, we will use the following general definitions:

- **The War Generations** (born before 1946). Often referred to as "the Greatest Generation," this rapidly dwindling group came of age during World War I, World War II, and the Korean War; and the values they learned at home and at war profoundly shaped them. As a whole, they are frugal, loyal, and conservative.

- **Baby Boomers** (born 1946-1964). The War Generations gave birth to seventy-eight million Baby Boomers, a generation whose values were shaped by the turbulent 1960s and 1970s. They grew up during the Civil Rights movement, campus unrest, the hippy era, and the Vietnam War. They were consumers, but also creative entrepreneurs. By necessity of their large numbers, they started new businesses and made investments. As Boomers age and move from their productive years into retirement, their massive size will place tremendous strains on the economy and health care.

- **Generation X** (born 1965-1984). They are sometimes known as the Xers. As children of the Boomers, there are only sixty-nine million of them—nine million fewer Xers than Boomers. This smaller generation has lived in the shadow of the Boomers, but will take over as Boomers head to retirement. Their smaller numbers mean that when it's their turn to pay the heavy taxes to keep the country running, they will be hard-pressed to do so.

- **The Millennials** (born 1985-2010). With an enormous population size of one hundred million, they will face workforce competition greater than previous generations have known and will be forced to start up new businesses to meet their needs. But they will meet a ready market, since they also consume an average of five times more than the Boomer generation.

Generational Giving Styles

The concept of multiple generations is as old as time itself. People of different age groups have been coexisting ever since we started having children. Today, however, the advances in technology have made the generational gaps more striking than ever. As technological changes continue to revolutionize society, each generation has grown up in a vastly different cultural and social environment. With unprecedented growth in social media and technology, gaping differences appear concerning why and how each generation gives. In order to reach the different generations with your fundraising campaigns, you first need to understand their different preferences.

- Those in the **War Generations** lived most of their lives before computers were commonplace, and they still prefer traditional direct mail as their primary means of solicitation. Organizations garnered this demographic's support through relationships. They met with them directly over a cup of coffee or dinner, seeking to build a friendship with the donor through these meetings. This was an effective method, since lifetime support often resulted from those relationships. These givers will be loyal and will likely even include the charity in their will.

- Many **Boomers** still prefer direct mail but are increasing their online giving as well. Unlike their parents, they are moving away from lifelong giving commitments and moving toward occasional gifts that bring a high return on investment. They wish nonprofits with similar missions would collaborate instead of compete with each other. They want to see tangible results, and they expect nonprofit organizations to sustain themselves.

- **Xers** are cause-motivated. They enjoy volunteering for or participating in a campaign or event more than their predecessors. They also tend to promote their causes via social media, and they rely on peer-to-peer influence.

- **Millennials** will likely donate online, even if contacted through direct mail. They want to be involved but have fewer dollars available to give. Once they grow older, however, at one hundred million strong, they will be a group to pay attention to. They respond to stories, not appeals for money, and they focus on causes more than results.

Implications from the Generations

Along with understanding the generations' giving patterns, it's important to be familiar with other aspects of their demographics. Although each generation's consumerism can be boiled down to "Larger generations buy more; smaller generations buy less," the same isn't necessarily true for their giving. Beyond size, a generation's giving can be influenced by multiple factors. Each generation's age, saving habits, entrepreneurial endeavors, and religious interests all play a role determining levels of giving. The factors are interrelated, affecting each other. Below are some factors you must pay attention to so that you know how to reach the generations.

America is Aging

Many of the organizations that exist today were built through the generosity of the War Generations. Although the term "the Greatest Generation" applies to their contributions during the World

Wars, it also aptly describes their giving habits. They are savers, but they are also dedicated supporters. They give generously and faithfully. They are as loyal to nonprofits as they are to their families and their workplaces. But as they age and become unable to give, this staple of nonprofit revenue is disappearing.

The War Generations have retired and are passing away. Between the War Generations and the Boomers who have already retired, more than forty-five million Americans are sixty-five or older. That number will grow as fifty million more Boomers age into retirement. What does the graying of America mean for nonprofits? It means the bread and butter of giving will soon disappear from the table.

Because the War and Boomer generations are aging, nonprofit organizations need to have a dual focus. First, they need to reach out to aging givers to cultivate planned giving and estate gifts. Second, nonprofits need to get serious about finding ways to draw in younger givers. A new generation of givers needs a new message.

Wealth Will Change Hands

As the current older population ages and retires, America will undergo arguably the biggest wealth transfer of all time. As we shared previously, an estimated $40 trillion dollars will pass from one generation to the next by 2050.

The passing of the War Generations will drive part of this wealth transfer as they pass on and leave their wealth to heirs. Boomers will drive an additional part as they head into retirement and eventually pass away.

Business Sales Will Bring Opportunity

Throughout the past half century, Boomers flooded the market as unprecedented consumers. As a result, new business opportunities sprang up, and Boomers started new businesses to meet the increasing consumer needs of their own generation. In addition, Boomers started businesses in a climate primed for growth. The internet was exploding, and the business world was becoming more and more globalized. At the same time, the world wars were long over and the economy was growing. Their businesses prospered. Boomers had a larger-than-ever generation and, as a result, started more businesses than ever.

Now as the Boomers head for retirement, they are poised to sell or transfer ownership. Over 65 percent of them will sell their businesses within the next ten years.[1] Those business sales will drive even more giving, because the Boomers won't leave all the proceeds to their children. They'll want to leave a portion to charity. Anytime a business owner sells a business, this is a golden opportunity for a major gift to your nonprofit. We'll cover connecting with major donors more in Chapter Four.

The Giving Population Will Shrink

Just as great opportunity lies with Boomers' aging, so does great concern. Approximately ten thousand Boomers turn sixty-five each day[2] and subsequently head toward retirement. After they reach their retirement years and their paychecks give way to pension plans, their giving will diminish. The Boomers will be replaced by a much smaller Generation X. The math is simple: Fewer people equal fewer dollars.

Taxes Will Rise

As the Boomers head to retirement, the smaller generation of sixty-nine million Xers simply won't be able to sustain seventy-eight million Boomers needing Social Security benefits. On top of needing to support the exploding elderly population, Xers will also need to fill in the gap on taxes that the Boomers used to pay. The burden of supporting the elderly and a government accustomed to high revenue from Boomer tax payments will put a squeeze on Generation X's income. Although there will be one hundred million Millennials, they won't be able to help, at least not for a few decades. While they're still young and getting their financial feet under them, they won't be able to bear all the government debt and unfunded entitlements (such as Medicare, Social Security, and federal employee's future retirement benefits) which *The Wall Street Journal* has estimated at $86 trillion.[3] The only way for the government to even begin addressing such liability will be through tax increases. Tax increases will inevitably mean less disposable income and less giving for Generation X and those that follow.

Demand for Services Will Increase

While the pool of taxpayers shrinks, the aging population will grow. This growth will place a greater demand on charitable programs for the elderly. Charities will be stretched thin with demand for their services, and they'll need increased giving to be able to meet the growing need. Unfortunately, their need for help will come when the supply of resources is at an all-time low, since Xers will be hard-pressed with higher taxes. There will be more pressure for charities to offer their services, but less resources for them to do so.

Religious Interest Is Down

Statistically, people with religious affiliations are more likely to give to charity, regardless of whether charities are faith-based or not.[4] But a declining interest in religion will mean a declining motivation for future generations to give. We are seeing today what some refer to as the rise of the "nones"—those who, when asked to claim a religious affiliation, mark "none." They claim no religion as their own. The Millennials are by far the least religious generation. In the War Generations, only a small margin was unaffiliated, but this number has increased with each generation, hitting 30 percent with the Millennials.[5] As the former givers age out, a new generation will replace them, one with less religious connection and therefore less motivation to give.

Revolutionary Focus

With the upcoming wealth transfer as Boomers and War Generations age, coupled with the population explosion of Millennials, the next twenty years hold unprecedented potential for fundraising. Yet the next twenty years will also require a dual focus. First, nonprofits must emphasize capturing major gifts. They must reach older donors with a planned giving focus and reach Boomer donors with a major-gift approach. If they don't focus on the older generations, nonprofits will miss the opportunity of a lifetime. Second, as their historic donors disappear, nonprofits must be diligent in attracting younger givers who will eventually replace the current older generations of donors.

The days of a shotgun approach to marketing are over. In a world of changing generations, strategic use of technology and the ability to capture new forms of gifts will be essential.

CHAPTER ONE

Questions

1. Which generation has given most consistently to your organization in recent years? Which has given the least?

2. Do you take a "one-size-fits-all" approach to marketing, or do you tailor communications to the specific generation you are trying to reach?

3. Which generation or generations will be most critical to the continued success of your organization?

4. Do you have a strategy in place for helping your organization benefit from the ongoing transfer of wealth?

My Action Steps:

_____

_____

_____

_____

_____

_____

_____

_____

_____

TREND TWO

The Technology Boom and Online Giving

"Automation applied to an inefficient
operation will magnify the inefficiency."
BILL GATES

In 1994, during the infant days of the internet, a writer for *Wired* magazine predicted, "In the years to come, most human exchange will be virtual rather than physical, consisting not of stuff but the stuff of which dreams are made." Today, over twenty years later, his predictions are surprisingly accurate. As texts, emails, and social media messages flit through the airwaves and pop up on our phones, we hardly think twice about the scope to which digital exchanges dominate our lives.

As demographic trends shape the future of giving, technology stands as the largest current phenomenon. No other force has changed culture—let alone giving—like technology. It has erased limitations of time and distance in our communications. It has also made mass publishing over blog or social media sites essentially cost-free. With this increase of technology, nonprofit organizations must realize that they cannot approach fundraising strategies the same old way. They can't rely on a telephone database when landlines are disappearing. They can't send out long letters to reach a web-saturated audience, especially one with the attention span of a 140-character tweet.

Old methods don't work anymore. In the past, direct mail served as the dominant form of solicitation. A nonprofit organization would send out a letter, provide a response card, and encourage people to send in a check. For today's donors, however, direct mail presents some obstacles. Donors need the letter, the response card and the check all in the same place at the same time, which, in our busy world, is less common than you might imagine. Millennials might not even own a stamp or a checkbook. Response rates have dropped as unsolicited mail piles up. And as the cost of postage continues to climb, each piece of unopened mail takes a toll on the bottom line. Even a significant number of donors who open their paper mail choose to give online.

This decline doesn't mean that direct mail is going away as a form of fundraising. It won't, as long as the older generations keep giving in this way. But it won't produce the same results it did in the past. As new generations raised on iPhones come of age, nonprofits will have to focus more and more on online fundraising as a central mechanism of giving.

The first step to cashing in on the technology trend is to be online. But being online is only the beginning. Through integrating your system to receive different forms of payment, using technology to create advocates, and opening up to mobile givers, you'll find yourself connecting seamlessly with a new generation of donors.

The Future of Online Giving

The internet has saturated society, and online gifts are following this trend. From 2015 to 2016, charitable gifts from online giving increased 7.9 percent.[1] If this rate of growth stayed the same, by 2035, online contributions would reach 30 percent (perhaps more) of all giving. This means that out of the total donation pool of roughly $300 billion in annual giving, online gifts would account for $100 billion.

As online giving grows in acceptance and as we move toward an increasingly younger donor base, the percentage of online giving will only increase.

Being Online Is Not Enough

While online giving is on the rise, it still only accounts for 10 percent of total charitable gifts. And according to a 2015 report by Decision Analyst, most nonprofits are dissatisfied with the online experience they offer their donors. Adapting to the rise of online giving means more than adding a credit card page to a website. Adapting also means adopting entirely new marketing strategies that allow you to live in the same online spaces as your donors. Donors live in their email inboxes, waiting for another email push from you. They live in social media, expecting two-way communication with you and telling all their friends about you the moment you make an impact. A credit card page is simply a rudimentary beginning.

When the online giving world first started, the old methodolgy was to create a website, usually nothing more than a full-color bro-

29

chure online. From there, the nonprofit organization might add a credit card page. Eventually, they would add an email newsletter provider and blast out newsletters to the organization's entire address list. This approach was essentially doing direct mail online.

As social media grew, we saw organizations take the step of adding Facebook and LinkedIn pages. Some had videos, so they posted them on YouTube or Vimeo. Some joined the mobile scene and added text-based giving as well. But generally speaking, most organizations lacked any fundamental unifying approach to their online pieces. Each of these activities—their website, credit card page, Facebook page, emails, etc.—stood as separate silos with no connection to each other. Worse yet, each of these strategies were often executed by separate outside companies using different user interfaces and thus varying customer experiences.

Finally, nonprofit organizations found themselves becoming technology integrators (connecting different parts and pieces of technology) instead of focusing upon doing the work they were passionate about. If an organization could afford it, they hired an IT director, but even this role became overloaded as IT directors were forced to work in more than their expertise. They had to know everything about the organization's website, social media, digital marketing, and mobile apps, all of which could quickly become overwhelming. An independent study commissioned by iDonate revealed that many nonprofits have as many as five fundraising platforms they're trying to manage. This disconnected approach to online fundraising won't work for today's donors.

Systems that Work

The key to success in online fundraising is to have all your methods of communication tied together in one single system. The old method of fundraising allowed for departmental silos. The present and future will not allow it. The high number of nonprofits in the

US competing for limited donations forces them to use technology well. Unfortunately, according to Decision Analyst, over 60 percent of nonprofits reported not having their systems integrated.

Lack of integration causes two problems. First, it gives donors multiple experiences as they move across different ways of giving (whether by a text, at an event, on a web page or through a mobile app). This can confuse them and cause anxiety. Second, lack of integration creates multiple data silos that have to be reconciled, managed, and exported or imported to multiple systems. This process is very costly and time-consuming for a nonprofit, and makes it difficult to evaluate how much these systems are really costing your organization. Furthermore, it's difficult to have one holistic picture of each donor's giving experience. (We'll discuss data silos more in depth in Chapter Three.)

To avoid confusion, you've got to maintain consistent, simple user interfaces throughout every mode of communication—your website, credit card page, social media profile, etc. A single key message supporting the veracity of your organization must be woven throughout your different platforms. The message must have emotional pull while providing hard and fast data support-ing the results of the mission.

The emotional pull often comes through stories that tie your organization's impact to the donor's gift. The underlying software for the online giving system must allow for this kind of consistent thread. Increasingly, nonprofits will move away from patching together different systems such as database management, credit card processing, text giving, publicly traded stock, and planned giving. Instead they will move toward one integrated software platform that provides multiple giving solutions. One such sys-tem is iDonate, which Ray Gary and I started to free up nonprof-its' time. We wanted ministries to be able to focus on what they were good at—ministry—and let the system do all the techni-cal work for them. iDonate is the only platform in the country that offers an integrated online giving system. It allows for both cash and noncash giving, and it also tracks donors' online giving activity.

An integrated platform is necessary because it allows organizations the ability to test different approaches and observe people's reactions. As a nonprofit, you need to have the tools and metrics to know if your online experience works for your donors. Whether tracking key words, click-throughs, conversion rates, average donation sizes, web traffic or other metrics, to be online means you need to measure and constantly calibrate. In the online giving space, testing is essential and also much easier to accomplish.

An email campaign can be crafted with control groups. Each control group may receive a different message, and the response to those messages can be tracked. This testing allows for more precise messaging and produces a higher return on investment.

Indeed, nonprofits will increasingly seek to let their systems do the work for them instead of building and integrating multiple systems. By doing so, they'll spend more time on their primary mission.

When successful nonprofit organizations tap into this approach, they'll find that they actually have more time for the nonprofit work to which they've been called.

Creating Online Advocates

The real shift in the online giving space is to move away from an online transactional experience to an online advocacy experience. The focus is not on contact management systems that merely manipulate data. Frankly, managing donor data becomes irrelevant if it doesn't lead to a gift. Instead, you'll want your website to create a space where potential donors can meet you and learn more about your cause. Focus on the donor's experience, and make your technology decisions based on their needs.

When you're switching technologies, you need to make sure the technology is market-driven, or "outside-in." Don't just leave all the technology decisions to the IT department. Far too many nonprofits have made managing donor data their emphasis instead of creating an online experience.

It's all about the relationships you form with your donors. Today's Millennials want to know who you are and what you're about. When they visit your website, 88 percent will click on your "about us" page first.[3] Make sure it's relevant and up to date. Fifty-one percent will then connect with you via social media,[4] so make sure your social media is just that—social.

Tami Heim, president and CEO of Christian Leadership Alliance, offers suggestions for using social media: "As practitioners in the social media space, we find very few ministries that really know how to engage that space, to communicate well in it, and to really be relational." Heim shares that being relational means supporting others. For example, if you set up a Twitter account, don't just post about yourself and try to rack up followers. Follow other people's causes related to yours and retweet their posts.[5] Tell your story in a way that engages people and encourages them to follow you.

Being relational also means creating online advocates. When Millennials connect with your nonprofit's cause in a personal way, they'll post about it, telling your story over and over. Having a third party praise you online builds your credibility, so acknowledge your advocate's value. Share their posts on your profile (if appropriate to your cause), send a thank you note or small gift, ask them to be a guest blogger, or invite them to special events your organization hosts.[6] Advocates are especially helpful since peer fundraising is a huge influencer for Millennials, according to the Millennial Impact Report. Seventy percent of Millennials are willing to raise money on behalf of a nonprofit they care about,[7] so make sure you're tapping into their networking potential. Remember, it's all about the relationship.

In the book *Facebook Era*, Clara Shih, CEO and founder of Hearsay Social, a social media marketing company, offers advice for how organizations can "take the digital plunge." The first step is to start wherever you are. Social media is a forgiving space, and the sooner you start, the sooner you'll grow comfortable with this new form of media. Engage your organization's leadership in what you're doing, and build your community of "fans." Social media is an easy way to track who's interested in your organization's cause, with page visits, likes, and reposts all providing instant feedback. Make sure you're integrating social media for more than marketing and brand awareness; instead, use it to engage donors, volunteers and ambassadors.[8]

Going Mobile

As you're engaging donors online, remember that they're most likely interacting with you from their phones, since over half of all web traffic comes through mobile devices. The average American spends thirty-two hours online a month,[9] with over half of that internet use coming from a mobile device. And this mobile trend isn't just for the young. Although 90 percent of Americans ages eighteen to thirty-four own a smartphone, older adults are quickly closing the gap on this trend at 76 percent.[10]

The Millennial Generation in particular sees mobile phones as enhancing the quality of their lives by making work easier, allowing them to manage time better, and bringing family and friends closer. According to *USA Today*, nearly "90 percent of Millennials say their phones never leave their sides."[11]

Not only do they use their phones for web browsing; a study by Blackbaud found that when Millennials give, 62 percent of them give through their phones,[12] using a website, app, or text-giving. And with a 200 percent growth rate, mobile donations are poised to become the giving medium of the future. Your organization must be prepared to receive gifts the way donors want to give them.

In preparing to receive mobile gifts, make sure your giving page is set up to be easily viewed through a smartphone. If it is not, few users will have the patience for it. Construct your mobile giving page in a way that mirrors your website, without making the user "pinch and zoom" to read the page.

A variety of mobile giving apps exist that allow users to set up giving accounts. Some of the most popular ones are GoFundMe and Tilt, which allow users to raise funds on behalf of different causes. Crowdfunding apps are gaining in popularity with the Millennial generation because Millennials can source their social networks to raise money for a specific campaign without having to jump through the hoops of fundraising with a larger organization. Most in this generation don't like the idea of giving to general funds but would rather raise money for something specific.

Texting is also a popular form of giving, and it's an effective means to reach people since 90 percent of texts are read within three minutes.[13] To give through texting, the user sets up an account, then simply enters the giving code with an amount. Texting is growing in popularity with younger generations that prefer a simple and portable way of giving.

Whatever mobile mediums you set up, make sure you're integrating them into one seamless giving experience.

Making the Change

Historically, many nonprofits have shied away from fully embracing technology. It's expensive and time-consuming to develop new methods when the old ones have worked for years. But doing things the old way won't work for much longer. Technology is here to stay, and the organizations that will thrive are those that will embrace the change and look for new ways to connect with new donors.

Making these changes will set you up for success: Make sure that you offer a meaningful experience online. Tie donors to your cause by interacting with them and helping them to become online advocates for your cause. Instead of having separate systems for different giving options, integrate these options into one streamlined system that unites them all. Recognize that today's younger generations eat, sleep, and breathe smartphones, so be prepared to interact with them through this medium. Become mobile-friendly if you're not already. When you embrace all these changes, you'll find yourself prepared to receive the next generation of givers.

* * *

CHAPTER TWO

Questions

1. On a scale of one to ten, how would you rate your organization's implementation of new technology?

2. Do you make the internet, email and other technology centerpieces of fundraising, or do you view them as add-on's to conventional tactics?

3. When is the last time you freshened up the look or updated the content of your website?

4. How are you tracking conversations taking place about your organization? Are those conversations generating gifts?

My Action Steps:

_____

_____

_____

_____

_____

_____

_____

_____

TREND THREE

Finding Donors through Data

"In God we trust; all others must bring data."
W. EDWARDS DEMING

Lincoln Memorial University doubled their donations from two million to four million in just one year. They didn't hire any new fundraisers. They didn't spend any new money on more events or more mailings. They simply used data.

Data analytics is the ability we now have to store mass amounts of information digitally and glean knowledge from it. Since the information is digitized, we can interact with it in new ways and learn from it in order to make smarter decisions when reaching out to our donors. We have at our fingertips an ever-growing pool of donor information that can tell us what works, what doesn't, and where to find new donors. It's all in the data.

Lincoln Memorial University's journey into data began with one of their alumni, Charles Holland. After graduating, he started QualPro, a consulting company that has spent over thirty years working with hundreds of organizations by teaching them to test new approaches using statistical analyses. QualPro helps companies analyze what works and what doesn't, and then do more of what works. As an alumnus to Lincoln Memorial, Holland decided to offer his company's services for free. He helped them test new fundraising ideas, like taking a yearbook along when they went to visit a donor or changing when they sent out appeal letters. Through analyzing their donor data to see what worked and what didn't, they learned to ask the right people at the right time using the right method. Today, Lincoln Memorial's donations have reached nearly $7 million, thanks to using data.[1]

Out with the Old

Traditionally, nonprofits stored data using a customer relationship management (CRM) system that was flat. It had paragraphs of hand-typed notes that had to be sifted through manually. A fundraiser might make a note on a contact record that read, "Susie Donor is forty-eight, works at the floral shop, and gave fifty dollars during our annual pledge drive." However, none of this information would be accessible by a computer. It had to be read by a person. When multiplied by hundreds or thousands, these records would be impossible to sift through. No fundraiser could use them to find meaningful commonalities regarding their donors. Because organizations couldn't analyze their information, fundraising was a shot in the dark. Flat CRM systems offered little insight into donors' giving patterns and provided no way to analyze the information as a whole.

In with the New

Along with the digital age has come the ability to store data digitally. For the first time in history, we can interact with stored information. This means we can ask it questions through algorithms, and it answers. Corporate America has been using this for years. For example, Target knows that if a woman buys large quantities of items such as unscented lotion, cotton balls, and vitamins, she is in her second trimester of pregnancy. They've analyzed their consumer purchase records to a T. From this information, they can predict her due date, send her maternity coupons, and be the first store to capture her new-mom brand loyalty, just from their data.[2]

Target isn't the only store keeping track of purchases. Every company keeps track, if they're smart. For every person in the US, there is a growing collection of information on them, including where they live, where they work, and what they buy. The massive buildup of this data has been termed "big data." Big data is a marketing term referring to the scale of digital information available online. It has grown to the point that no person on earth understands its full scope, and it is still growing by the minute. Data is revolutionizing the world, and nonprofits can benefit from it.

Data can be used by nonprofits to focus marketing efforts and make informed decisions. It allows you to ask questions about your donors, such as "Who are the best donors in our organization?"

Data allows you to see where the patterns are with your donor base and where you should focus your fundraising efforts. It takes out the guesswork. Now that data is digitized, you can interact with it in new ways. No longer is data just for corporate marketers. It's taking over the nonprofit world, too, helping you be smarter and savvier about where to target your fundraising efforts.

Using Data

As a former lawyer, I love data. If a case was going to succeed, it had to be built on facts. I rarely had previous knowledge about the topic I was defending, so I would go and collect data to support my case. There's nothing like cold hard facts to guarantee an outcome. Having information turns your hunch into a fact worth acting upon.

Nonprofits can do the same with data. They can either build their fundraising on hunches and guesses, or they can turn to the facts to make wise decisions in fundraising. According to Wealth

Engine blogger Mike Lee, key areas for using data to benefit your nonprofit include timing, affinity, and resources.

Timing—Lee shares the story of walking out of a James Bond movie, wanting to be as cool as James Bond. He suddenly needed every product shown in the movie, from the Omega watch to the well-tailored suit to the new car. If a retailer had set up a James Bond kiosk outside the theater, he would have bought everything on the spot.

Marketing is all about catching the consumer in the moment. People have to be in the right mood to give up their hard-earned money. The same is true for fundraising. Take holiday giving, for example. Every fundraiser knows donors are more likely to give during the end of the year, but when exactly is the best time to ask? Do you push all your fundraising efforts onto Giving Tuesday? Or do you wait till those critical days after Christmas but before the end of year tax cutoff date? Using data to track responses helps you to send out appeals at the ideal time.

Affinity—Know what people care about. Data can provide information on where they work, what charities they give to, where they donate their time, and what kind of products they buy. Looking holistically at your donors can help you pinpoint the best way to reach them. For example, if your donors love the outdoors, why not fundraise by hosting a nature walk? Or partner with an outdoor supply store, agreeing a certain percentage of donors' purchases will go toward your charity. Use data to know your donors and appeal to them in a meaningful way.

Resources—Through data, you can know your donors' capacity to give. They may have only given a twenty-five-dollar gift to your organization but actually have thousands available to give. They only need to see the importance of your cause to be motivated to give more. However, as a fundraiser, you cannot possibly have the time to personally connect with every donor who gives a small gift. That's where data comes in. Having a wealth intelligence resource such as Wealth Engine can help you sort through your donors to find which ones are the most strategic to pursue.

Organizations need to start using data in two main ways. First, they need to be using their internal data, the information they already have on donors. This means tracking the people who have already given to the organization. Second, they need to start using big data, a large-scale collection of information combined from other companies and used to find new donors or new information on current donors.

Internal Donor Data

Tim Sawer, vice president of marketing at World Vision, uses internal data to track the performance of their child sponsorship television commercials. World Vision used to air their commercials late at night since this time slot cost less than daytime and still had a high response rate. Because of the response rate, Sawer thought the commercials were effective. However, as he tracked those donors' giving over time, he saw that the donors who responded to late-night ads had a higher likelihood of canceling their sponsorships than the average donor, and their giving lessened over time. Sawer realized that although these ads had a high response rate, they didn't have a high rate of return on investment. So World Vision switched to the costlier daytime ads, realizing it would gain them more money and provide a higher return in the long run.

Keeping track of your fundraising performance helps you to target your efforts where they're most effective. Use test groups to know what works and what doesn't. Lincoln Memorial, the university referred to at the beginning of this chapter, tried over two dozen different fundraising ideas to see what worked and what didn't. This helped them to make smart choices about how to fundraise. The stats showed that when they used a yearbook, sent out a wish list for donations, or shortened the pitch letter in their appeal, giving increased. However, sending out a photograph of a brand new dormitory actually decreased donations, probably because it was nicer than the facilities the alumni used when they attended the university. As the fundraisers tried new ideas, the morale on their fundraising team increased. Seeing what actually worked empowered them to have confidence as they went out fundraising. No more guessing. The stats were in.

Avoiding Data Silos

As you analyze your data, remember that your analysis is only as good as the data you collect. Leigh Kessler, Charity Engine's chief of marketing, warns nonprofits about the danger of siloed data. If each department chooses their software based on whatever need they have, they can easily create data silos. For example, the marketing team needs to send out emails, so they use MailChimp or Constant Contact. The events team needs to keep track of guests for the annual fundraising gala, so they use Eventbrite. The contributions team needs to record donations, so they use DonorPro. If your team already cares about data, each department might keep track of its own statistics—how many people opened each email, who attended the gala, and who gave a donation in the past year. But when it comes time to analyze the data as a whole, they can't. It's all in separate storage, or "silos."

"They have all this data in all these places, and they can't make sense of it," says Kessler. "They can't use it, it's repetitive, it's redundant, it's wrong."[3] To remedy this separation of data, an organization needs to focus not on which software is easiest to use or best for each department, but on what is best for the donor. Your organization's data needs to be in one spot to give the most holistic view of a donor. Only then will you recognize your superstar donors—the ones who attended the marathon, raised money from friends and family, volunteered at your community service project, etc. Don't let them fall through the cracks.

Software options like iDonate or Charity Engine bring all your data under one system. Programs like these allow you to reach your donor base in a unified manner and let those donors know how important they are to your organization. In an ad by Charity Engine, Terry Shoemaker shares the example of "Mary Donor" who for years registers for an annual charity walk, creates a peer-to-peer fundraising page, and recruits friends to donate. Clearly, she is dedicated to the cause. Yet in a traditional siloed database, if she hadn't donated any gifts herself, she might continue to receive appeals for giving or even worse, a lapsed-donor letter lamenting that she hasn't contributed in so long. But with a unified database, the nonprofit can recognize her contribution to the organization and give her the thanks she deserves.

Data Cooperatives

Barbara was a lawyer. She had a huge heart for animals and for children. She'd left her entire estate to the local animal sanctuary. She volunteered with a local orphanage. When she received a letter from Save the Children, it tugged on her compassionate heart because it addressed topics she was already passionate about— serving the underprivileged and taking care of the helpless. She had never given to Save the Children before, but because of the letter, she donated $250. Barbara found a new cause to support, and Save the Children found a new donor. Save the Children knew to contact her because they had just joined the Abacus cooperative, a data co-op that pairs nonprofits with new donors.[4]

Barbara's story illustrates the effectiveness of data co-ops. Data co-ops are growing in popularity as nonprofits search for ways to find new donors. An article in *The Chronicle of Philanthropy* explains how data co-ops work: In order to join a co-op such as

Abacus, a nonprofit must share a list of donor names. The nonprofit gives the co-op information about donors' giving habits such as how much they gave and when. The nonprofit then pays a fee, and in return, receives new names from the co-op's database. The names are by no means random. Sophisticated algorithms sort through giver statistics to select those most likely to donate to a certain cause.[5] By being strategic about whom they solicit, nonprofits can save money on fundraising campaigns and bring in more money than ever before.

There are about six firms running major nonprofit cooperatives, including DonorBase, Epsilon, Wiland, and Apogee. Apogee's vice president, Matthew Frattura, shared that their database contains 1.1 billion charitable transactions from 66 million donors. But the data isn't just limited to charity. They combine charitable information with a larger shopper database. That database contains information on over two hundred million Americans, "roughly equivalent to the entire consumer public."[6] The most meaningful data, however, is provided by nonprofits.

According to Robert Reger, senior vice president of Epsilon, co-ops provide nonprofits with three main services. First, they help with name acquisition, bringing in new donors that will likely give long term. Second, they help lapsed donors start giving again. And third, they run marginal lists through an optimization process, separating names of donors that would be likely to give from donors that wouldn't.[7]

Data cooperatives can even track connections to potential major donors. For example, The Henry Ford museum in Michigan wanted a major company in the area to sponsor its education program. The only problem? No one at the museum actually knew anyone from that company. Luckily, though, the museum subscribed to a database that tracked relational connections. Through data, the museum discovered that one of their trustees' former colleagues now worked for the company. A few introductions from the trustee and the colleague, a meeting with top executives, and voila, a year later the company made a six-figure gift.[8]

Although we can't promise every attempt will end that successfully, relational data tracking increases the likelihood of a gift, since people give to people they know and trust.

Does a Co-op Break Donor Trust?

Some nonprofits are worried that if they give donors' names to a data cooperative, this will betray the trust of their donors. In response to this concern, Frattura shared the story of a children's welfare charity who decided to test how joining Apogee, a data co-op, would affect donor relationships. The charity took one hundred thousand of their existing donors and split them in half. One group they submitted to Apogee's database, which would expose those donors to significantly more promotional material. The other group remained unexposed. For two years, the charity compared the two groups' results. The charity feared that once donors were exposed to more solicitations, they would either find new organizations to give to and end up giving less to the first charity, or they would get frustrated by the amount of new mailings and stop giving to the charity altogether. However, after two years of testing, the charity found no difference in donor behavior. Each group performed exactly the same. No donors disappeared. No one gave less because their names had been shared.[9]

Brent Eskew, executive vice president for sales and marketing at Wiland, claims that nonprofits have little other option than to share names. Before the financial pressure of the 2008 recession forced nonprofits to turn to new methods to find donors, nonprofits would do traditional list exchanges, giving lists directly to each other without going through a third party. However, Eskew says this method is now outdated. "Nonprofits that have relied really heavily on list exchanges have tapped out those sources and seen their universes shrink," according to Eskew.[10] After the recession, data co-ops paved the way as a ready avenue for finding new donors, one that provided a bigger pool and higher efficiency.

Time and again, nonprofits that use data co-ops are seeing that the benefit is worth it. "The reason nonprofits are participating is because it's working," says Allison Porter, president of Avalon Consulting, a direct marketing agency in Washington D.C. "We keep analyzing the return on investing and saying, 'Is it still worth it?' And it is."[11]

On the other hand, one legitimate worry is a loss of control. Anytime you give your list of donors to anyone outside your organization, you lose control of those names. That's why it's important to be careful where you trade. Check ahead of time how the co-op protects donor privacy, and whether they will resell data to a third party.

Also, remember that name-trading is nothing new. Nonprofit organizations have been trading names for a long time. It's just growing more sophisticated now with the availability of data. Regardless of whether you participate in a data co-op or not, your donors' data is already in circulation. Their names, demographics, and consumer transactions are all easily accessible to outside companies, and you're only adding a small piece of the pie—their giving habits for your specific charity.

Take the Data Plunge

Implementing data can seem like a huge task, especially if you haven't been tracking it. Start by making sure you have a system that allows all your data from events, marketing, and donations to be stored in one spot, such as iDonate. It takes time to build up data, so be patient. Once you have a good chunk of data, it's time to analyze it. Look for commonalities between your big donors, and use that information as you decide who to target for finding your next big donors.

If you want, you can even bring in an outside specialist to help you analyze. Once you feel that you can consistently use your own data, you will want to take the next step of joining a co-op. Using outside resources might be costly, but they will pay off in the long run as you increase your donor base and learn to target your marketing budget to where it will pay off the most.

The numbers aren't just numbers. Data tells stories—stories of how donors respond and what they respond to. Listening to your data equals listening to your donors. It will pay off. As you listen to them, they will feel known and valued.

* * *

CHAPTER THREE

Questions

1. Does your organization have one database to track all your interactions with donors, or is your data siloed into separate software?

2. What characteristics do your major donors have in common? If you're not sure, how do you plan to find out?

3. How can you use data to recognize your donors' overall service, beyond their monetary gifts?

4. What could your organization gain by joining a data cooperative?

My Action Steps:

_____

_____

_____

_____

_____

_____

_____

_____

TREND FOUR

The Crucial Major Donor

"I don't have time for major donor
relationships. I'm too busy with the ministry."
AN ANONYMOUS NONPROFIT LEADER

When I started in the nonprofit world, frankly, I didn't have any substantial fundraising experience. I was a lawyer. I knew fees, not gifts. And so I learned as I went. In the early days of The Signatry, we didn't aim to raise support from lots of people but instead sought support from a handful of stakeholders. In particular, two people gave significant gifts to get us started. As the years went by, we thankfully discovered that this approach was, in fact, the best approach. Within four years we owned our own building and had established a significant presence in our city.

I can't say this more pointedly: you must emphasize and cultivate your major donor relationships. While every donor matters, your major donors determine your organization's survival. The principle of the major donor is nothing new, but some major demographic shifts make focusing on major donors even more important in today's fundraising world.

Demographic Shifts to Major Donors

As we've already pointed out, the demographics tell us that the next twenty years are perhaps the greatest time for major gifts in the history of our country, with $40 trillion passing from one generation to the next. More specifically, Baby Boomers will inherit an estimated $14 to $20 trillion during the next twenty years. This transfer of money holds significant potential for major gifts.

"This is something that will never happen again," said Brent Bouchez, founder of Agency Five-0, a company that markets to consumers over age fifty. "What's more, this group will probably not leave a lot of that money to the next generation."[1] The Boomers have wealth, and they're not leaving it all to their kids. They want to give a substantial amount to charity, but they need you to show them how.

Additionally, ten thousand Boomers turn sixty-five every day, many with a substantial ability to make a major gift. According to CNBC, the average millionaire is sixty-two years old.[2] They've worked their whole lives to save money for a comfortable retirement. Now that they've retired, instead of being in a saving mindset, they're ready to give. As these wealthy Boomers grow older and retire, they will pass on their wealth, and only some of it will go to their kids. The rest will either go to taxes or to nonprofits.

This wealth transfer and opportunity for major gifts will only last for a short time. Currently Boomers and the War Generations are the biggest givers. After the War Generations have passed, the Boomers have retired, and the Generation Xers have become the dominant generation, giving will drop. There are simply not enough Generation Xers to fill the giving void left from the nearly eighty million Boomers retiring. But within the next twenty to thirty years, we have a brief window of opportunity to capitalize on the greatest wealth transfer in history. The only way to take advantage of it is by reaching major donors.

Although major donors have been hurt by a sagging economy, they still have the resources to make major gifts. Middle-income givers, on the other hand, have been more negatively affected by the economy and the market. As unemployment, market losses, and higher costs of living squeeze the middle class's finances, they're left with less cash to spare than before. So with middle-income givers facing so much financial pressure, it's more important than ever to focus on major donors, those who have the capacity to give and who have recovered quicker from the economic crash.

In summary, major donors can alter your organization's course. One large gift from a major donor can equal hundreds of small gifts from middle-income donors—an entire year's worth of efforts. While no person and no income is insignificant (we've seen people on fixed incomes make six-figure gifts), in general, some people have greater abilities than others to give through their finances. High-income givers are skilled at accumulating wealth and want to use it for the greater good.

Changing the Paradigm

Some organizations will read this and admit that they've neglected major donor relationships, either because they don't have time or because they're too intimidated to talk to them. Some will say they don't have any major donors. Others will read this and think they're doing just fine. For any of these views, we'd like to change your paradigm by showing both the prevalence of major donors and the insufficiency of most nonprofits' major donor strategies.

The Reality of Major Donors

For those organizations that have placed little emphasis on major donors, we would encourage you to begin focusing on reaching them. If you think you don't know any major donors, here are a few statistics to consider:

- Ten percent of Americans control 75 percent of the wealth.[3]

- Close to 11,000 households have net assets of more than $100 million.

- Another 115,000 households have net assets greater than $25 million.[4]

Let's define terms:

- **High-capacity givers** are people with household incomes of $200,000 or more. Approximately 4 percent of US households are in this category.[5]

- **Middle-income givers** are people with annual household incomes from $75,000 to $199,000. Approximately 28 percent of US households fit in this category.[6]

With this many high net worth families, chances are you're closer to major donors than you thought. You just have to meet them.

Who Are the Major Donors?

Get rid of the mindset that you can spot a major donor off the street. According to Thomas J. Stanley's *The Millionaire Next Door*, wealthy people usually look just like the rest of us. Stanley tells of meeting a thirty-five-year-old Texas millionaire who owned a successful business rebuilding diesel engines. When they met, Stanley mistook him for one of the truck drivers. He didn't look like a millionaire. He wore old jeans and a buckskin shirt, drove a ten-year-old car, and lived in a lower-middle-class neighborhood alongside "postal clerks, firemen, and mechanics." He was a millionaire, but you never would have known it by looking at him. Stanley tells this story to illustrate that oftentimes the wealthy aren't into status symbols like a $5,000 watch or a foreign-made luxury car. They "live below their means, wear inexpensive suits, and drive American-made cars."[7]

Don't assume you can recognize someone's income by their lifestyle. Instead, realize that finding a major donor can be much more systematic. Major donors typically fall into one of several categories:

1. Core Business Owners—business owners who started a business and grew it over time. These businesses will typically have fifty-plus employees and will provide a steady source of support for the owner and family.

2. Serial Entrepreneurs—business owners who have a creative itch. They start a business, sell it, and then start another one. Or they start and run a few businesses at the same time.

3. Professionals and Executives—doctors, lawyers, accountants, etc., who fall within a higher income bracket. Or they may be executives within companies, including publicly traded companies, but not necessarily owners.

4. Retirees and Halftimers—retirees who have received inheritances or built personal wealth over time to have the luxury of retiring. Halftimers are young retirees who have sold a business and have enough personal wealth to retire early. They're usually looking for ways to invest their assets.

Obviously, there can be other categories of major donors, including highly compensated sales professionals, heirs of second or third generation wealth, professional athletes, and private foundations. But these four main categories can help take the mystery out of who the major donors are.

How to Reach Major Donors

Before I started a nonprofit, I practiced law for twelve years. I was a member of a sizable law firm. Since every lawyer has to bill their hours, all of my time was spent in the office. I knew our lawyers, a few of the clients and a few of the judges, but I didn't know my community outside of the four walls of our law firm. However, when I switched to nonprofit work, I realized I needed to get out and meet people. I didn't know anyone. My only resources were my car and my cell phone, so I started from ground zero.

Do Your Research

Instead of instantly going out to meet people, I actually sequestered myself so that I could research. Research might seem counterintuitive because it's not a social activity, but it's actually the most important place to start. I researched the top churches in the area, top nonprofits, top businesses, and top business owners. Then, as I went into the community and met people, I recognized right away if someone knew a person I had read about. Or I would ask if they knew any of the people I'd read about. From there, I could ask to be introduced.

Do the research to discover the business leaders in your area. Read business journals to find lists of top business owners, physicians, law firms, etc. These will give you a list of people to meet. Also pay attention to those who are starting new businesses and hiring employees. Find CEO forums, and then offer to be a guest speaker for them on an issue you're knowledgeable about. For example, if you're a youth minister, offer to speak to them about issues youth in the community are facing and what business leaders can do to address these issues. Watch for business or real estate owners on the verge of a sale, who will be looking for ways to relieve their tax burden. The people are out there; you just have to do a little homework and networking.

In networking, use online media as a resource for connecting with people. I spend an hour a day on LinkedIn to find new people, and have found this a helpful tool in my research. If I find someone who looks promising, I'll send them a message asking if they'd like to meet with me. If you're going to be an online presence, make sure you clean up your profile, including your website and your social media profiles such as Facebook and LinkedIn. People will look at your online presence as many as seven times before they talk with you, so make sure it accurately reflects who you are. Make sure your profile is inviting and polished for people who are exploring your nonprofit.

Once you've found people you want to meet, the next step is the introduction. The best way to meet a high-end giver is through an introduction from someone who already knows them, such as a board member, existing donor, or financial advisor. (See Chapter Ten for ideas on networking with financial advisors.) Use social media as a tool for figuring out which relationships you have in common with major donors. And when you finally do meet them, don't just limit yourself to talking about your nonprofit. Brainstorm what information would be useful to the major donor, find people they would like to meet, and offer your knowledge to them.

Become an Authority

You don't want to always have to seek out people. Eventually, you want them to seek you out. Become an authority on giving. Research your community to find out what the median level of giving is, the median income, the total income, and the impact that increased giving could have on your city. For example, when I first started researching, I found that in the Kansas City Metro area, if giving were to go up by 2 percent, giving would increase by $800 million. Knowing statistics like these establishes you as an authority on giving. Once you're an authority, people will seek you out for your expertise and will give you a platform later on down the road.

I once received a phone call from a man who had just returned from a trip to Haiti. During his time in Haiti he had been inspired by what he saw and wanted to give in new ways by using business and charity for his cause. Upon returning to the US, he asked around our city to find out who he should talk to about new ideas for generosity. People kept suggesting he talk to me. After he heard my name enough times, he finally called me, and that first phone call led to many seven-figure gifts. He came to me because I had developed a reputation of being a generosity connoisseur.

Challenge Them

As the nonprofit world changes, so does the kind of fundraising personality it takes to achieve success. Some nonprofits used to call it "friend-raising" and sought to hire people solely good at building relationships. Salesforce, an online customer relationship management platform, recently completed a study applicable to the fundraising world—the top successful sales profiles. The study showed that the sales profile most people perceived to be the most successful was the Building Relationships Profile. In reality, this profile ranked the lowest. The highest-ranking profile was what Salesforce called the Challenger Profile. People in this profile had the ability to cast a big vision, provide challenge and insight to potential customers (or in our case, to major donors), and move them to a different perspective.[8]

Provide Value

For those of you who think you have a good handle on major donor relationships, it might be time to rethink your methodology. First of all, don't approach them as people who have something you need. Recognize that when you reach out to them, you have an opportunity to serve them. A major donor is always a two-way relationship. They have something to offer you, and you have much to offer them.

Keep in mind that today's major donors have literally hundreds of choices of where to donate. I know of one major donor who sold his business, and as soon as word became public of the sale, was besieged with nonprofits who suddenly wanted to talk to him. Because donors have so many choices, fundraisers must provide value to the major donor. You need to have a reason for a major donor to want to meet with you, more than just being a nice person. Bring value, advice, information, or insight to the table.

Know Their Financial Needs

To reach major donors, we have to understand their needs. Although most organizations seek cash gifts, the majority of major donors' wealth is in noncash assets. They're business owners, real estate owners, collectors, and estate holders. There is both need and opportunity here, since major donors are concerned with how to deal with these noncash assets, especially in regard to taxes. In many cases, their first and primary issue is reducing income tax. Income tax reduction through charitable giving, particularly through giving noncash assets, becomes very attractive.

One of the most significant opportunities comes in the context of a business owner selling a business. When a business is sold, the government locks in capital gains taxes that can amount to millions of dollars. But if the business owner gives company stock as a charitable gift before the sale, they can cut their tax bill while substantially increasing their giving. When a donor sells a business, this is an excellent opportunity for a nonprofit to help the donor save on taxes by donating to charity. Unfortunately, it is also one of the most frequently missed opportunities. When nonprofits discover a donor selling a business, they should always seek to learn whether the business owner has addressed the tax issues and charitable giving opportunities.

Here's how this scenario played out for a nonprofit I worked with: Our friend Joe ran a small private school of two hundred students. He knew that his friend Steve was considering selling his business, so Joe introduced Steve to a charitable tax planning expert with the The Signatry. It was just the right time. Steve confided to the tax expert that he was getting ready to sell his business, and in a matter of weeks Steve completed a gift of 3 percent of his stock. A few months later, Steve sold the company, and this small school which had never received a gift larger than $10,000 now received a million-dollar gift. Steve and Joe's story is just one example of the many ways nonprofits can reach out to major donors regarding their noncash assets. We've found that by simply asking about this pain point, we've received millions of dollars. The key is to connect with donors at the point of opportunity.

And donors have needs that go beyond taxes. Donors need to be encouraged to give—not for the sake of your organization, but for the good of the donor. Studies show that generous people lead more satisfying and purposeful lives, but they might need you to challenge them to do so.

With great wealth comes high responsibility. Donors have worries. They might be paying extremely high income tax, wondering who will get their business when they're gone, or questioning how to leave a family legacy. You are there to help them, or at least to connect them with tax lawyers, financial advisors, and other people who can help.

Remember They're Human

I grew up as a poor kid on the wrong side of the tracks. My family ate corn bread and beans every day, and I wore hand-me-downs from my older brother. Fast forward to the present, and here I am working with billionaires. (God must have a sense of humor.) Having seen life on both ends of the spectrum, I can tell you that it isn't all that different. Every person has the same needs deep down—to feel loved and significant. As you get to know your donors' stories, learn to see beyond their income and into their lives.

One example of this is my friend Morton. A nonprofit leader first introduced me to Morton, hoping that he would make a gift to that leader's organization. But when I talked with Morton, I quickly moved beyond his high-figure income and saw a lonely man who had been married five times and was currently estranged from all his kids. As we talked, I realized that his biggest needs were friendship and help in working out the issues of his estate. He wasn't close to his kids and didn't want to leave any part of the estate to them. I befriended Morton, and as we continued to meet, I encouraged him to include his children. Eventually Morton agreed with me and included them in his will, but because of our friendship, he also ended up passing on the bulk of his multi-million-dollar estate to charity.

With Morton, my connecting with him in his moment of pain was more important than any gift he gave. Because I was able to help him with his need, we connected on a deep level.

There are many like Morton, people who have big needs. Don't assume they have it all together just because they have money. Dig deep enough to uncover where the hurt is, and be there to serve them. They'll build relationships with you when you connect with them on an emotional level.

Seize the Hour

The window of opportunity is wide open at the moment, but we must enter in before it slides shut. How much time do we have?

With this unprecedented opportunity, leaders must act to capitalize on the potential gifts. And they must learn to be effective in reaching this wealth, including tapping into the wealth that lies in donors' noncash assets.

CHAPTER FOUR

Questions

1. Has your organization ever made a concerted effort to reach major donors as part of your fundraising strategy?

2. How can you identify potential major donors in your community or those with an interest in your mission?

3. After knowing major donors' expectations, how would you tailor your story to appeal to them?

4. How would you explain to your board, and other donors, your emphasis on major donor contributions?

5. How would a major donor benefit from your fundraising strategy?

My Action Steps:

_____

_____

_____

_____

_____

_____

_____

_____

TREND FIVE

The Growth of Noncash Giving

"Start where you are. Use what you have.
Do what you can."
ARTHUR ASHE

When I first started The Signatry* in 2000, I'd just left a position in a prestigious law firm. There, I had my own secretary, paralegals, document clerks, copy clerks, and messengers. Now I was a one-person shop. After a few months, I hired my first employee and became a two-person shop.

Our primary focus was on serving nonprofits and providing them with resources. A unique part of our work for the The Signatry was handling gifts of real estate and closely-held business assets. These gifts tended to be $500,000 or more. But nonprofits would also call us asking if we could handle some unusual gift for them, like a 1967 Buick hardtop or a timeshare in Aruba. We were too naive to say no, and we tried to figure out how to take those gifts. We found out it was really hard, time-consuming, and unproductive. We learned to start saying no when these requests came in. However, it turned out that these requests came in a lot. As we reconsidered whether we could say yes, we stumbled on a key fact: most of America's wealth is in noncash assets. This means that people don't just have endless bank accounts filled with cash. They've invested their money in stocks, businesses, real estate, and an endless array of other items (as we would soon discover).

* *In 2000, we started out with the name "Christian Community Foundation in Kansas City," now called "The Signatry."*

As we looked deeper for solutions, we experienced a turning point. One of our key nonprofit partners, a church, called us. They were afraid. They were getting ready to launch a capital campaign, and their pastor was going to ask for all kinds of non-cash gifts. Knowing full well that their church did not have the resources to handle these gifts, they begged us to handle the gifts for them. Now, I've never claimed to be the brightest guy, but it occurred to me that for years now nonprofits had been begging us for this kind of help. People wanted to donate noncash gifts, but organizations weren't equipped to receive them. If it was a problem, there had to be a solution, and an opportunity.

We agreed to help the church, and so began a long process of figuring out how to accept noncash gifts. Eventually, we hired a retired marine to come on staff with us at The Signatry. Good thing he was tough, because he had to bust his head against the wall time and again to find a solution for these nonprofits. After a few trials and errors, we figured out that we could build a web-based solution where we could handle noncash gifts online. We would receive the gift, sell it for cash, and then pass on the money to whichever charity the donor chose. Then we realized we could embed this process directly in a nonprofit's website and process all their giving for them. And thus, iDonate was born—the country's first comprehensive giving solution handling cash and non-cash gifts in a single platform.

We made lots of mistakes. But eventually we worked out the kinks, and we started to pick up traction. The best move I ever made was to hire someone a whole lot smarter than I am—Ray Gary. Gary had a background in technology and in scaling businesses, and we both wanted to do something big to help nonprofits. Eventually Gary took over iDonate, and he is now the CEO.

The business, iDonate, was born because we were continually flooded with requests for processing noncash gifts. After receiving enough of them, we finally got tired of turning these gifts down and found creative ways to receive them. Getting so many offers of noncash donations caused us to ask, why do so many donors want to give noncash items?

Majority of Wealth is Noncash

Donors want to give noncash items because that's what they have. According to the Boston Foundation, over 95 percent of America's wealth is in noncash assets.[1] When I read this statistic, an obvious question came to mind: Why do nonprofits only ask for cash? Eighty percent or more of their donations come as cash, even though 95 percent of the wealth is noncash. By only asking for cash, traditional fundraising tactics completely ignore the majority of potential donations. Over two million nonprofits exist in the US They all go fishing in the same overcrowded pond of cash donations, while right next to them is an ocean of noncash gifts, teeming with potential but essentially ignored. We need to start receiving people's wealth in the form it's already in and stop expecting them to do the hard work of conversion for us.

When we talk about gifts of noncash assets, we're not talking about donations such as food or supplies that will be used by a charity. We're talking about assets that will be sold to produce cash. If a donor owns something that can be converted to cash, it has value to your organization. Here are just a few ideas to spur your imagination:

- Businesses

- Real estate

- Cars, RVs and boats

- Stocks and bonds

- Jewelry

- Art or coin collections

- Designer purses and scarves

- Grain

- Old business inventory

- Electronics

- Mobile phones

- Estate assets

People give what they know and what they understand. The single largest form of giving in the country is cash, which makes sense, since we deal with it daily and have done so since childhood. It's manageable and clear cut. Cash is easy to exchange, as simple as handing over a bill or punching in credit card numbers. The next largest form of giving is publicly traded stock, which typically represents $20 billion of annual giving. This form is a little more difficult, since giving stock involves brokers, paperwork, and strategic timing of the gift for when the stock is most valuable. But stock is still straightforward and accessible enough to be given fairly often. Oddly enough, the next most common form of giving is planned gifts through estates. However, a planned gift is the hardest to give, since you've got to die first in order to give it!

While cash, stock, and planned gifts are most commonly given, other potential gifts slip by unclaimed—things like cars, phones, and real estate. In theory, all of these gifts would be highly valuable to a nonprofit organization. The problem, though, is that they're difficult to donate. For example, if someone were to simply drop off their old RV in your organization's parking lot tomorrow, what would you do? You'd probably be more inconvenienced than grateful. Why? Because you're not equipped to handle it. The trouble of getting the title, transferring ownership, and liquidating the gift would all feel like more trouble than it was worth. So while people have these items and may want to give them, most charities aren't set up to receive them.

In short, it's time to rethink our philosophy, not just about giving but about what should and can be given.

Why Pursue Noncash Donations

There's huge incentive to pursue noncash donations. Noncash will be the giving of the future—an untapped source of income. The increase of goods and the transfer of wealth make it more important than ever to pursue these donations. Let's dive deeper into reasons why.

Americans Own a Lot of Stuff

Americans, especially Baby Boomers, love their stuff. Minimalist blogger Joshua Becker shares astounding facts on how much stuff Americans have. For instance, according to the *LA Times,* the average home has three hundred thousand items, ranging from paper clips to that big-screen TV. With all this stuff, it makes sense that in the past fifty years, home sizes have more than doubled.[2] After all, we need somewhere to place all those items. You'd think that with all this extra space, Americans would have enough room to store all their stuff, but that's not the case. One fourth of people with two-car garages don't actually have any room in their garages to park a car—it's used as storage space. Another one-third only have room to squeeze in one vehicle in that double-wide garage, according to the US Department of Energy.

And apparently, even garages aren't enough space. Self-storage units have been one of the fastest-growing sectors in US real estate, with one in eleven US households renting a self-storage unit.[3] The US has over fifty thousand storage facilities, more than five times the number of Starbucks. According to the Self Storage Association, there is currently 7.3 square feet of self-storage space for every person in the nation. Thus, every man, woman, and child could stand—all at the same time—under the canopy of self-storage.[4] We could literally house our entire population in self-storage units.

Americans own so much that they don't have a place to put it. It's spilling out of their houses into their garages and from their garages into self-storage. As older generations begin downsizing, let's help them put their stuff to good use by providing a way for them to donate it.

Generations Will Pass on Wealth

At iDonate, the Billy Graham Evangelistic Association is one of the ministries that partners with us. We'll process non-cash donations for them and then send them the proceeds check. We received a request one day from a woman whose mother had passed away. The daughter had a problem. She had inherited sixty-two Madame Alexander dolls—her mother's entire collection, worth hundreds of dollars. The problem? She didn't want the dolls. She didn't care about dolls. They were her mom's passion, not hers. She wanted to get rid of them. Thankfully, she decided to donate them to the Billy Graham Evangelistic Association. We sold them, and the association received a $900 donation.

More than 95 percent of our nation's wealth is in noncash assets, and who owns those valuable assets? The oldest generations—the War Generations and Baby Boomers. Their assets come in the form of anything from dolls to yachts to Longaberger baskets. Over the next ten years, as the War Generations pass, they will leave estate assets behind. These estate assets are valuables that will be sold or passed on to family. Or, if you're strategic, they can be left to your nonprofit.

A huge chunk of America's assets are also owned by the seventy-eight million Baby Boomers, with the most economically powerful being those on the leading edge, the Alpha Boomers (born 1946-65). They've spent the past fifty years starting businesses, investing profits, saving for retirement, and buying excessive amounts of stuff. Now, as they enter retirement, they own more property, more vacation homes, more businesses, and more luxury vehicles than any other demographic. And as they continue to grow older, these asset-laden Americans will begin to divest their holdings, in part to fund their retirement, but also as a way to give back to their communities and their society. Their beneficiaries will be their heirs, the government, or nonprofits.

At the same time, their kids—the Gen Xers and Millennials—don't want to inherit their parents' stuff. They have a different lifestyle and a different set of values. Boomers are downsizing and trying to pass on their stuff to their kids, but the kids don't want it. They don't have room for the family pool table or eight-person dining set in their downtown flat. They see the emptiness of their parents' endless accumulation and are opting for a simpler lifestyle.

Auctioneer Stephanie Kenyon shares how the market is saturated with old Boomer items that younger generations rejected. "Hardly a day goes by that we don't get calls from people who want to sell a big dining room set or bedroom suite because nobody in the family wants it," she says. "Millennials don't want brown furniture, rocking chairs or silver-plated tea sets. Millennials don't polish silver."[5] In short, Millennials don't want their parents' stuff. They're design-conscious, they value mobility, and they don't want to be burdened with stuff they don't need.

Instead of selling these unwanted items or sending them to the dump, why not donate them to charity? Setting up your nonprofit to receive these donations will benefit both you and your donor. You'll receive more donations, and donors will have an easy way to get rid of unwanted items. Also, they'll feel better about giving family heirlooms to a cause they believe in rather than to an unknown auctioneer or to the junkyard.

The Economy Encourages Noncash Giving

Another reason to encourage noncash donations is that, in an unpredictable market and economy, these gifts maintain their stability. Following the crash of 2008, people and corporations sensed the squeeze on cash. As the economy plunged to depths unseen since the Great Depression, people began to get nervous about their own financial stability. Even if they didn't personally lose money because of the crash, they felt inclined to hold on to it for safekeeping. For nonprofits the result of all this was that cash giving went down. However, the resourceful donors began giving their noncash assets. During the aftermath of the crash, even as cash donations went down, corporations actually increased their noncash giving.[6] In fact, according to the Center for Effective Collaboration and Practice, "Noncash continues to account for the majority of [corporate] giving growth in the past decade."[7] When the economy tanked, noncash gifts floated to the surface as a viable giving option, one where donors would not feel as much of a loss after giving.

And people have become creative with their gifts. Since the 2008 recession, we've seen several unusual gifts at The Signatry. Someone once donated a hearse; another donated an Andy Griffith squad car replica. We've also received the more common gifts like artwork, RVs, and old vehicles. All these gifts had value. Never underestimate donors' creativity and desire to help. Even in a down market, they'll find ways to support their favorite causes. If you're able to receive it, they're willing to give it.

Less Competition for Noncash Gifts

Most nonprofits don't ask for noncash gifts. As we mentioned, 80 percent of donations come in the form of cash, even though cash makes up only 5 percent of America's total wealth. Because the majority of giving in America still comes in cash, noncash giving is wide open. No one else is asking for that timeshare in Aruba or that hardwood oak dining set. They don't think of asking their donors to rummage through closets for old cell phones or computers. However, when nonprofit organizations start accepting noncash donations, they will quickly ramp up donations. iDonate has seen that, on average, when nonprofits start accepting all kinds of donations, their gift size increases on average by 250 percent, more than doubling what they were bringing in previously. This increase shows that there is great wealth available, but most nonprofits are not tapping into it.

Helping Major Donors

As we pointed out in the last chapter, major donors have noncash assets. They own businesses, real estate, artwork, cars, second homes, airplanes, etc. By being able to receive noncash gifts, you can often solve a problem for a major donor by accepting an item they want to get rid of, and you can gain their loyalty in the process.

Many people have valuable items, but they don't have the means to transport them. After retiring fifteen years ago, one farmer's tractors were still sitting out in his fields. Then he heard that a nonprofit could benefit from them. He donated them to Rio Grande Bible Institute. He received a free haul-away for his unused tractors, and the school received over $2,000 in proceeds.

Another man, an entrepreneur, wanted to get rid of a statue. He had originally set out to start a jewelry business and had purchased jewelry as inventory. Unfortunately, someone convinced him that raw gems were far more valuable than jewelry since the stones were more easily liquidated. So he traded his jewelry for the gems. Then another person said that instead of raw gems, he should trade the gems for a 700 carat ruby-laden statue of Ganesh, the Hindu god of success, appraised at $200,000. He agreed and made the trade. Sadly, the appraisal was false, and the man was swindled out of his inventory. Later on, he decided to donate the statue simply to get rid of the reminder of his bad experience. In the end, the statue was sold for seventy dollars, and the proceeds donated to East-West Ministries International, a ministry that works in Hindu countries.

In addition to helping donors get rid of unwanted items, there are also tax benefits for giving noncash gifts. A few years ago, The Signatry worked with two real estate developers. The developers sold a piece of property and received a significant amount of proceeds, which produced major tax implications for them. However, they realized they had a second parcel of real estate they could donate that would offset their tax liabilities. We handled the real estate gift, and one of the developers became a board member!

We gained their trust by meeting a need. Noncash donations don't just help you; they help major donors by lowering their tax burden and relieving them of unwanted items.

Start Now with Noncash Donations

The ability to market and receive noncash donations is part of the new fundraising revolution. As the War Generations pass on and the Boomers downsize, never before has there been such a vast number of unwanted items—valuable items that could benefit your nonprofit. And in a shaky economy with an unpredictable market, one where donors feel the need to save their dollars for a rainy day, noncash giving provides a risk-free alternative. Even more, it's this kind of creativity and innovation in accepting gifts that impresses the giving world and produces engagement. For the donors, it encourages them to see their stuff as more than just possessions—these things are a way to impact the world. No longer is their old stuff just taking up space in a garage or storage unit; it's now being used for a good cause. As donors give their goods, they can see tangible impact—a return on investment.

* * *

CHAPTER FIVE
Questions

1. What percentage of your organization's contributions are in the form of noncash assets? Has this number changed in recent years?

2. Have you considered increasing your emphasis on noncash contributions, or do you feel that it would be too much of a hassle?

3. When you talk with potential donors, do you discuss the tax implications of their gift as well as the benefits to your organization?

4. Do you have processes in place to accept noncash contributions and liquidate them?

My Action Steps:

_____

_____

_____

_____

_____

_____

_____

TREND SIX

The ROI Emphasis

"Don't tell people your plans. Show them your results."
ANONYMOUS

Writing out my annual check to the IRS always triggers doubts about how our government handles money. Now don't get me wrong. I'm all for the "Give to Caesar what is Caesar's" philosophy, and I believe we should support our government. But when it comes to my hard-earned dollars, I want to know they're being spent well. Frankly, I'm not always sure that's the case with Uncle Sam. I wonder, as April 15 rolls around, will my tax check go to something noble, such as fulfilling a constitutional mandate and defending the nation, or will it be used to build a bridge to nowhere in a powerful senator's home state? Giving away my money feels like giving away a part of myself, and I want it to go toward a cause I believe in.

Today's donors—especially major donors—want to know the same: where their money is going. More and more nonprofits are springing up, making it more necessary than ever to build a convincing case for why a donor should give to your organization. According to Steven Lawry, senior research fellow at Harvard's Hauser Center, "Donors want to be assured that the charities they support are working as effectively as they possibly can."[1] With limited assets and unlimited sources of information, donors have become more sophisticated and more discerning about who receives their money. And with tens of thousands of potential nonprofits to donate to, they will search for a nonprofit that best fits their values and expectations. As a nonprofit leader, you must assure donors that their money is being used effectively by showing return on investment (ROI). Show them the results of their donation.

The Investor Donor

The other night I had a friend over—a missionary-hopeful on his way to New Zealand. Before he could move to this new country, he had to raise enough funds to live there. I invited him over for dinner to hear about what he was doing and decide whether I wanted to donate. As he shared over dinner his hopes of going to New Zealand, I started asking him questions about his future work. I realized very quickly that he didn't have a plan. He hadn't researched what the current spiritual climate of the country was. He didn't know how he would go about starting a church once he got there. He didn't even have a plan for how long he would stay before returning to the US. His presentation included lots of passion and hope, and even stunning pictures of New Zealand's landscape. But when it came down to what he would actually accomplish by going to New Zealand, it was clear he had no concrete plans. I enjoyed his stories, thanked him for his presentation, and saved my dollars for a different cause.

Unfortunately, this young man is just one example of many fundraisers who lack clear goals or knowledge of what the return will be on their donors' investments. With so many nonprofits vying for a limited donor pool, ministries can't afford to be vague in what they hope to accomplish or are currently accomplishing. The competition is too fierce for vagueness.

Many donors view themselves as investors and choose their charity with the same care an investor puts into buying new stock. In the book *Charity Case: How the Nonprofit Community*

Can Stand Up for Itself, Dan Pallotta, a nonprofit worker for over twenty years, advises donors to ask an organization these three questions before contributing:

- What are your goals?

- How are you progressing toward those goals?

- How do you measure your progress?[2]

Knowing donors will be asking these questions, nonprofits should take care to address them. These are excellent questions for nonprofit leaders to ask about their organizations so that they can provide clear information to donors on the impact of their gifts.

What are your goals? As a nonprofit, you should be able to provide your donors with clear-cut objectives that spell out what you hope to accomplish. Make sure you have tangible goals. For example, if you work with kids in the inner city, your goal should be clearer than a statement such as "Helping inner city kids." Your goal needs to be clear and specific, something concrete that gives direction. What kind of help are you going to provide? Are you going to provide nutritious food, educational help, or low-cost housing? A better goal would be: "Help inner city kids by improving their literacy rates." Be specific in defining your goal.

How are you progressing? Once you have a goal, you can look at your progress toward this goal. Continuing with the example above, if you want to improve literacy rates, what are you doing to get there? Offering after-school tutoring, hosting reading clinics, providing meet-the-author events and giving away free books would all be ways that you could show your donors how you are progressing toward your overall goal of improving inner city kids' literacy rates.

How do you measure your progress? Finally, make sure your goal is measurable. It needs to be tangible enough to hang numbers on. In the case of literacy rates, you would start out with a statistic of literacy rates before your program. For example, you might state, "Before our program took off, only 74 percent of students at Oak Creek Elementary were reading at grade level. Today, after conducting our afterschool reading clubs for two years, 84 percent of students are reading at grade level." These numbers offer a measure of how well the nonprofit is succeeding at its goal. This gives donors a concrete knowledge of what your nonprofit has accomplished.

If my friend who was headed to New Zealand had taken the time to answer these questions about his ministry—what his goal was, how he would progress toward that goal, and how he would measure his success—it would have gone a long way in helping him raise money to actually make it overseas.

New Generations, New Expectations

While each generation carefully invests in charity, each one has a different level of commitment. As a whole, the younger generations tend to be less loyal than the older generations. The War Generations expected to get a job and work there for life. Younger generations now expect to work for multiple employers as they climb up the career ladder. The same level of loyalty is expressed with their giving. The War Generations tended to find a charitable cause and support it for life. After them came the Boomers, who wanted to see results before they committed their loyalty. And finally, among the Xers and the Millennials, the average time of support has dwindled. These youngest generations will only support a charity as long as they can see a return on their investment. If your nonprofit is not yielding clear results, they'll switch to one that is.

And today's donors define results differently than those in the past. They want to know their gifts are making a real difference.

They want to give to organizations that support people and causes, not just buildings or a general operating fund. They are moved by stories of changed lives.

For example, the American Bible Society, a nonprofit that's been in the US for two hundred years, used to measure their impact by the number of Bibles they distributed. But as any nonprofit who has been around that long knows, you need to adapt reporting for new times. Now they measure their impact by the number of lives they've changed. Their website advertises, "The Bible is changing lives and communities worldwide," and offers stories to back up this claim—stories like that of Ameer, a Syrian refugee who received trauma healing at a retreat center sponsored by the American Bible Society, or Kiho, a ten-year-old Ugandan who had been abandoned by his mother and found hope through a class put on by the American Bible Society. These examples of changed lives are what today's donors expect to see. The stories equal impact. For the American Bible Society, it's not about the number of Bibles distributed, it's about the people affected by those Bibles. How does your nonprofit change lives?

Expected Transparency

Overall, the expectation of accountability has heightened as the nonprofit world becomes more transparent. The internet has made it easy for donors to gain info about your organization's finances. Donors can go online and pull a tax return for most any organization through services like Guidestar.org. They can see staff incomes, track expenses, and view bank amounts.

Since many donors view themselves as investors, they want to know that you're being responsible with their money, not spending it on frivolous expenses. They don't want full-color brochures or expensive thank-you gifts. They want simple, one-page statements that, frankly, look a lot like investment reports. These statements should quickly explain the organization's vision, mission, goals, and accomplishments, as well as what the donor's gift will yield.

As part of this increasing emphasis on return, watchdog groups like Charity Navigator and Charity Watch have sprung up. These organizations routinely investigate charities and report on things like how they're doing financially, how transparent they are with their finances, and how much of their budget goes toward their programs versus their overhead expenses. Similarly, because of social media, donors can instantly find out their peers' opinions about a particular organization. Be sure to watch your ratings in watchdog groups, and keep tabs on conversations online about your organization. If your ratings are low, find out what you need to do to improve them, and do it. This will take extra effort now, but it will pay off as you build your donors' level of trust.

With this heightened need for transparency, make sure your organization stands out as being excellent at making the most of your donations. Use donors' money well, and let the donors know how you're using it. Doctors Without Borders does an excellent job of transparency. When the 2004 tsunami hit South Asia, donations poured into the organization for relief efforts. After receiving sufficient funding, Doctors Without Borders announced they had received enough funds and would not accept anymore money specifically designated for relief efforts, which was an unprecedented move in fundraising. Today, Doctors Without Borders still offers to return specifically earmarked gifts that end up unused. According to their director of development, Thomas Kurmann, "Accountability and transparency—we live by those principles every day." This accountability and transparency has paid off. In the past fifteen years, Doctors Without Borders has grown from $50 million to $332 million.[3] Build donors' trust by self-reporting often and by being open with your finances.

One-to-One Impact

Many nonprofit leaders have fought against this notion of return on investment, but it is an idea that is here to stay. Donors have numerous choices and want to be wise stewards of their resources. With increasing competition from an ever-widening pool of nonprofits, each organization must be able to prove the worth of its work in order to win donors' confidence.

Every church, ministry or other nonprofit has a story of impact, but all too often, that story gets lost somewhere between the organization and the donor. In many cases, the cause seems so overwhelming that donors feel they can have little impact. One of the most powerful ways to remedy this problem is to show a one-to-one correlation between the gift and the result.

For example, if your nonprofit helps AIDS orphans in Africa, a donor might be tempted to think, "With hundreds of thousands of orphaned children, what can my gift possibly do?" In that situation, consider which of the following statements convinces a donor of the importance of a singular gift—that it can make a difference:

- Your gift of twenty-five dollars a month will help us meet the needs of African children orphaned by AIDS.

- Your gift of twenty-five dollars a month will provide housing, food, and education for one AIDS orphan in Africa.

Clearly the second, because it shows direct impact. In the first appeal, the twenty-five dollars disappeared into a vague pool of funds. But in the second, it went specifically to one child, one child that wouldn't receive basic life needs if it weren't for the donor's gift.

Although not a nonprofit, the company TOMS does an excellent job of showing impact. Their "One for One" slogan is about as simple as it can get. Their website homepage promises, "With every product you purchase, TOMS will help a person in need." If you buy one pair of shoes, they'll help provide one free pair to a child in need. Buy one pair of sunglasses and help one person regain their sight. Buy one item, help one person. The math is clear and compelling.

Compassion International also employs the one-to-one ratio. Instead of overwhelming the donor with the problem of worldwide poverty, they narrow the focus to making a difference in one child's life. When a donor signs up to sponsor a child through Compassion, the impact is clear: One donor's monthly gift of thirty-eight dollars will sponsor one child. This means that one child will receive food, clean water, clothing, and a quality education because of one person's gift. And their website takes the return on investment report a step further by featuring updates on the number of children who have been adopted, including video testimonials from the children themselves.

The equation of impact is essential, but it doesn't necessarily have to be a person impacted. The one-to-one impact can be applied to anything tangible. For example, through the National Wildlife Federation, one gift of thirty dollars allows givers to adopt ten acres of wildlife. At the Woodstock Sanctuary for Animals, donors' gifts are equated to a monthly sponsorship—ten dollars a month will sponsor a chicken, twenty-five dollars for a goat, and fifty dollars for a cow. In all of these cases, the donation actually goes into a generic pool of funds and is not specifically earmarked for one acre or one chicken. But attaching tangible items to dollar amounts helps donors understand how their gifts can make a practical difference.

Showing the Return

The bottom line is to communicate the bottom line. Show the results of your work in a meaningful way that donors can easily relate to. Remember that your donors have the same standards as investors. Just like investors, they carefully consider where their money goes and the return they'll gain from their investment. But unlike investing in the stock market, when they invest in your nonprofit, the results will be intangible. They want to see lives changed. They'll expect you to do this by delivering honest and effective work that brings results. If your donors are looking for changed lives, the most meaningful way to show this is through the one-to-one impact of their gifts. At the same time, they expect you to exhibit transparency as you communicate how their money is used. They are making an investment into your ministry and want to see results.

This new mindset of making investments will prod nonprofits to clearly report the difference they're making through donors' gifts. It will also encourage nonprofits to start creating real business enterprise, making a donor's investment more worthwhile.

* * *

CHAPTER SIX

Questions

1. Does your organization currently employ a simple equation that shows donors what their gifts accomplish?

2. If not, what value proposition would work best (for example, ten dollars a week provides one hot meal each day)?

3. If a donor asks, can you confidently and clearly explain how your organization measures its accomplishments?

My Action Steps:

_____

_____

_____

_____

_____

_____

_____

_____

_____

TREND SEVEN

Charities that Make Money

"Social entrepreneurs are not content just to
give a fish or teach how to fish. They will not rest until
they have revolutionized the fishing industry."

MUHAMMAD YUNUS

In 2017 *Inside Philanthropy* named impact investing one of the year's most promising trends in philanthropy.[1] So what exactly is this trend? And why is it so important?

A perfect example of impact investing is the Central Detroit Christian Community Development Corporation (CDC), started in Detroit over twenty years ago. In the 1970s and 1980s, Detroit was a city notorious for crime, and in 1994 CDC began as an effort to lower crime rates. They led parenting classes, youth sports and other events, doing whatever they could to help the city.

In its early years, the nonprofit lived from grant to grant, struggling to survive. "You always hope that the next grant is the one that takes you to the promised land, but it never does," said founder Lisa Johanon. In 2002, in an effort to generate new sources of income, they started something new: impact investing. Their first seedling business was a Tastee Freez franchise. It did well, and from there CDC grew more businesses, continuing to open businesses even during the recession years. Since 2002, they've started nine different businesses, ranging from a self-sustaining farm and fishery to a laundromat fitness center. Between 2008 and 2014, CDC more than tripled its revenue from businesses. However, these businesses don't exist just as side projects to create revenue for CDC. They play a key role in the heart of CDC's work.

The businesses strengthen the community, not just by providing jobs for an impoverished community but also through the products they sell. Their Fit & Fold Laundromat encourages physical fitness by providing workout equipment while customers wait for their laundry. In a neighborhood where there are twenty-three liquor stores for every one grocery store, the CDC Farm & Fishery brings fresh produce to the table. CDC is careful that each business provides a product that will enrich their community. These endeavors make CDC a prime example of impact investing.[2]

The Rockefeller Foundation coined the term impact investing to describe activities that both make money and have a social impact.[3] These enterprises are initially funded by capital, or gifts, until they begin earning revenue. That revenue is then used to support the nonprofit in some way. For CDC, grant money gave them the start they needed for impact investing, and their businesses now help sustain them.

Why We Need Impact Investing

For some, the trend of combining business with charity might be hard to swallow. After all, making profit can seem the opposite of "nonprofit." Traditionally, a nonprofit's primary goal was social benefit, and a for-profit organization's primary goal was making money. For-profit business owners and shareholders reaped the benefits of any profit earned, whereas when a nonprofit earned money, all profit went back into furthering the organization's cause. Because of this split, we've become accustomed to a deep chasm between profit and nonprofit, convinced that the two can never go hand in hand. Remember, though, this is a new world of fundraising. What worked in the past won't work in the future. Impact investing is needed for several reasons.

Disappearing Donor Base

Before, donors didn't mind supporting an organization for life. But today's donors view their gifts as investments. They want to be able to make one gift or a few gifts and know that those gift(s) produced results. They want their gift to allow the nonprofit to grow, gain its own income, become sustainable, and not require years of ongoing support. As one donor friend of mine said, "I don't like to make payments; I like to make gifts!"

Much of this change in mindset comes from a changing generation. As we discussed in Chapter 1, demographic shifts have revolutionized fundraising. It's safe to assume that donations to ministries will go down, both for new nonprofits just starting out and for existing nonprofits. Most donations currently come from a donor base age fifty and older. As these donors age, retire, and eventually pass away, they'll need to be replaced by a younger, equally enthusiastic donor base. Frankly, this isn't going to happen. The twenty-, thirty-, and forty-year-olds of today are not as enthusiastic about giving. They're burdened with debt and college loans. Moreover, they aren't religious like their parents or grandparents were. Since religious interest has been the driving motivation for donating to charity, they're not giving to charities like older generations have. Charities that have been around for one hundred years or more can't keep assuming they'll have a stable donor base in the years to come. As all their major donors age, they'll have a big problem. Their donor base will disappear, and they'll need to find new ways to sustain themselves.

Additionally, founder of Impact Foundation Aimee Minnich noted that younger generations, specifically Millennials, have an entirely different mindset when it comes to charity. They want to make an impact while they're making money.[4] In the past, older generations obtained a job, made an income, and then donated a portion of their income to charity. They focused solely on making money, and then when they had extra money beyond what they felt they needed, they donated that money to an organization. After all, social change was the job of charities and the government. Businesses made money. Charities helped people.

Not so with Millennials. They want to have financial success and make an impact at the same time. They don't see a dichotomy between work and charity. They want businesses to be socially responsible and at the same time be working to make a difference in the community. Older generations might have mental blocks when it comes to combining profit with charity, but Millennials are drawn to it. As one of Minnich's donors said, "Those over forty have a hard time understanding this; those under forty don't understand anything but this."

More Competition

While the donor pool is shrinking, the number of nonprofits is rising dramatically. In the US, the number of nonprofits has grown to over 2.3 million. That's a lot of nonprofits to compete against for a dwindling supply of donations.

Not only do nonprofits have to compete with each other for funds, but now they also have to compete with the trend of social businesses, or cause marketing. With cause marketing, when people make a purchase toward a cause, they feel like they've already given to charity, even if only a minimal percent of their purchase actually went to charity. For example, if a restaurant advertises that one dollar of each purchase will go toward a specified charity, when customers spend six dollars on a meal, they feel like they've made a donation. Then when a nonprofit comes and asks for a five-dollar donation, customers feel like they've already given six dollars. Higher competition and a shrinking donor pool are forcing nonprofits to find new ways to generate income.

Donors Want Social Responsibility

Moreover, the new generations of Xers and Millennials expect a new way of doing charity. No longer can charities simply give free handouts to the people they serve; the new generation expects full social responsibility by improving the economy and society as a whole. Donors view handouts as a dangerous method that fosters dependency. For example, after the earthquake in Haiti, Tyson Foods donated chicken to the disaster relief effort, and kept sending over crates of leftover chicken parts as donations. According to Minnich the first crate of free chicken quickly put local chicken farmers out of business.[5] Tyson intended to help, and did, but they didn't foresee the negative effects their handouts would have on the community. Charity must find the best solution to systemic issues, a solution that doesn't just patch up symptoms of social problems but offers answers that balance the many facets of the situation.

Impact Investing

With the changing demographics of donors, increased competition of nonprofits, and changing expectations of donors, nonprofits need to come up with new ways to fund their ventures. This is where impact investing comes in. It funds the nonprofit while at the same time serving its original purpose. It generates revenue while still serving the community.

A great example of impact investing is the Global Orphan Project. Originally created to help orphans, the Global Orphan Project saw that some supposedly orphaned children in Haiti would be picked up after a year or two by their birth mothers. These kids weren't actual orphans; they were economic orphans. Their parents would drop their children over the orphanage's wall and trust that someone would take care of them, temporarily abandoning them to the orphanage in hopes that the kids would receive food and education. So in addition to providing orphan care, Global Orphan started working on poverty, the root cause of abandoned children. They invested in local businesses, shipped the Haitians' products to the states, and provided a new market for local workers. Through impact investing, Global Orphan was not just giving handouts to orphans anymore, it was alleviating poverty.

Another illustration of impact investing is Seat King, a business started by Pete Ochs at a prison in Hutchinson, Kansas. Inmates work at the factory, a separate building within prison property, to produce custom-made seats for lawnmowers. Ochs started the business as a way to involve inmates in productive work, since he was convinced that beyond economic capital, a business should also create social and spiritual capital.

Seat King uses profit to enrich their employees' lives. They pay their workers $11 per hour, or $88 for an eight-hour day, a wage unheard of for inmates used to the prison's wage of 45 cents per day for work done at the prison. With this higher wage, inmates can afford the costly 17 cents per minute phone call home, an expensive and rare treat for other inmates not employed with Seat King. Seat King workers have also used their earnings to support their families and to pay for remote seminary classes, which have allowed them to start their first prison church pastored by inmates and not by an outside chaplain. But most importantly, Seat King fills inmates with pride in being able to live productive lives and take care of the people they love.[6] Ochs's business serves as an example of effectively using impact investing to make a sustainable difference.

For us at The Signatry, pursuing impact investing meant starting iDonate. At its conception, iDonate was solely a nonprofit that had been invested in through donations. As it grew, its success proved it was a concept that worked. Since iDonate was then earning money on its own, we converted it into a for-profit company. Now that it was a bona fide business, outside investors were willing to put money into it.

Every nonprofit has to get creative in finding its niche. For Global Orphan, this meant helping Haitian businesses. For Seat King, it meant employing prison inmates. For us, it meant serving ministries through an online giving platform. Find out what you're passionate about and discover how to turn your efforts into a sustainable business.

What Impact Investing Is Not:

Not Business as Mission

It's important to note that impact investing is not the same as business as mission (BAM). BAM began as a way to get missionaries into potentially hostile countries. Since some countries that outlawed missionaries would still allow a foreigner to enter the country to start a business, missionaries started coming in with businesses that they used as a platform to reach people. Sometimes these businesses aimed at strengthening the community through the business itself, and sometimes they provided a revenue stream that supported the missionary's activity. But the business always focused more on the people than the profit. These business missionaries were usually trained in theology, not business. Donors contributed to the startup costs, but often the businesses never reached sustainability.

While BAM does business as a missional effort, impact investing asks the question, "How can we make a profit?" It recognizes that profit is not an enemy of philanthropy, but rather, profit can help philanthropy. Business thinking can be very helpful, teaching nonprofits to use profit-making activities both to generate income and to further their mission.

The key difference between BAM and impact investing is that impact investing aims to make a profit while BAM is more focused on the people than the profit. BAM focuses on smaller projects where people are the sole mission, and it's not concerned with making a profit.

Not the End of Charity

While impact investing continues to rise as a solution, it will by no means eliminate charitable giving. Impact investing will supplement charities' donation income by providing alternative streams of revenue, but it will never replace donations. Giving, regardless of the availability of tax deductions, will continue. It may dwindle as the government becomes increasingly unfavorable toward charities (more on this in Chapter Nine), but it will still be present. Even as the younger generations become less religious and less inclined to give, people with compassionate and generous hearts will still give to those in need to advance causes they care about.

How to Start Your Impact

Those organizations seeking to move into revenue-generating activities can do so by taking a few practical steps. The first step is to recognize that revenue in addition to donations is not a bad thing. Nonprofits need to get rid of the false dichotomy between business and charity. "Profit" is not a dirty word, and business thinking can be very helpful in a charity context, as evidenced by CDC, Seat King, and the Global Orphan Project, to name a few. Moreover, younger generations expect charity and business to combine to create socially responsible endeavors.

Next, start looking for ways to generate earned revenue through your charity. For example, if you were a homeless rescue mission, you could start a thrift store that gave clothing to the homeless and sold clothing to the public, thereby creating revenue for the mission. Or if you wanted to wander a little farther from your charity's specific activities, you could find a donor who owned a business and ask that part of that business be donated to fund your charity. The sky is the limit in what your charity can do to generate revenue. Once you have an idea, here's how you can turn it into reality:

1. Bring together a strategic thinking team. As a nonprofit leader, as with any career, you likely have a few areas of expertise, and many areas in which you lack experience. You'll need people with other skill sets, a well-balanced team, to get your idea off the ground. Often this team will include business owners, but it may also include members with marketing, technology, and legal expertise. Creative, entrepreneurial people will help you work out the kinks in your idea and think through the various obstacles to your enterprise.

2. Be careful to avoid the naysayers. There's a difference between people who help you overcome obstacles and people who flat out reject your idea. Remember, what you're doing is new and different, and it may look scary to people from the outside. But starting a business always involves risk. In the early stages, you'll want to avoid those people who would be quick to say, "No, this will never work." Stick with the positive people who will work to provide solutions to potential problems.

3. Recognize that "a good plan working is better than one on the drawing board." Some call it the lean start up. Some call it failing fast. In any event, the idea is not to over-plan but to take a risk. It's better to get started, fail quickly, and then adjust to get to where you need to go.

4. Raise adequate capital. Starting a business involves risk and learning as you go, so make sure you've raised enough money to cover your mistakes and cushion the bumps in the road. Also, having adequate capital will allow you to hire high-quality people who will be the lifeblood of your successful business.

5. Choose the appropriate legal structure. Keep your business internal to your nonprofit only if it furthers an important aspect of your tax-exempt purpose. Also, keep in mind your board's willingness to innovate and take risks, as well as your donors' willingness to support the project. And of course, you'll want good legal and accounting counsel along the way.[7]

Impact investing can be an effective way to communicate your ROI to your donors. By following this trend of creating business as part of your charity, you're proving to donors that you're being responsible with their money. They have invested in you, and now you're turning around and investing their money in another enterprise.

***

CHAPTER SEVEN

Questions

1. Is your organization focusing on the sources of problems or simply treating the symptoms?

2. Have you been operating under the false dichotomy that business and charity have to stay separate?

3. How can you take the donations you're receiving currently and start making revenue for your organization?

4. Who would be on your dream team for planning this enterprise?

My Action Steps:

_____

_____

_____

_____

_____

_____

_____

_____

TREND EIGHT

Telling Stories that Show Impact

"The Great Stories are the ones you have
heard and want to hear again. The ones you can
enter anywhere and inhabit comfortably."
RON BLUE, KINGDOM ADVISORS

I remember speaking at a conference one time about the power of the story. I was trying to convey how storytelling was an important new trend. Some of the audience members nodded their heads, as if they had been ahead of this trend for years. "Ah yes, we believe in the power of storytelling," they said. And I realized I had not gotten my point across.

The trend is about so much more than telling a good story. There's little doubt that nonprofit organizations have been using storytelling for a long time. In fact, some organizations have lived off of one single story for the past twenty years—I say that a bit facetiously but not entirely.

The issue is more than storytelling. The trend requires your story to cut through the noise above all the other stories being told right now. You've got to tweak and re-tweak your message through multiple angles. Let's pause a moment and talk about the noise first.

More Noise

Dr. Seuss' *How the Grinch Stole Christmas* is my all-time favorite Christmas special. But do you remember why he hated Christmas? The Grinch bemoaned, "There's one thing I hate! All the noise! Noise! Noise! Noise!"

Do you ever feel that way? There are more nonprofits than ever. There are more communication methods than ever—text, Instagram, Facebook, Snapchat, email, direct mail, postcards, radio, television, etc. Today, donors are besieged by appeals. It feels like there's a bell-ringer on every corner, all clamoring for us to save the whales, save the trees, save the puppies, save the schools. And these are only the appeals from nonprofits!

People are constantly bombarded by advertising in general, whether by ads for cars, cosmetics, clothes, food, fitness plans, financial planning, etc. At every turn, someone wants their money. The noise is deafening. In order to survive, people learn to tune out the ads to maintain their sanity. Psychologists call this "selective attention." As humans, we can't possibly pay attention to every message being brought to us, so we listen only to what's important to us.

In this noisy world, the necessity of being able to tell a clear, concise, and moving story is critical. Nonprofits must be able to tell a story that separates them from the rest of the pack and allows them to rise above the noise.

Shorter Time to Connect

Not only is there more noise, but there is also a shorter timespan to grab donors' attention. Most of the information on the internet is created to be consumed in small chunks, which by nature caters to a shorter attention span and brief pieces of information. As donors scroll through their Facebook newsfeeds or glance at Twitter posts, your nonprofit message only has a few moments to grab donors' attention and convince them your cause is worth listening to. To succeed, you've got to draw them in within a few seconds.

Cutting Through the Noise with Your *Why*

The first place to cut through the noise is to know your *why*. Knowing your *why* is like the clink of a knife against crystal at a wedding—it gets everyone's attention.

I was at a lunch recently with a friend. He asked me about all the different ventures I was involved in. I drew a few of them out on paper. Finally, at one point, he leaned in and asked the question—really the key question, "Why are you doing this? Is it to make money? Is it just a good idea? *Why?*"

Without hesitation, I remarked, "I'm doing this because I believe we'll impact families around the country and for generations to come."

In a similar vein, he leaned further in and spoke with strength, "Now that's something I could be part of!"

Simon Sinek produced a popular video called "Start with Your Why." In the video, he describes the importance of communicating *why* you do what you do. According to Sinek, "People don't buy what you do; they buy *why* you do it."[1] To prove this theory, he used Apple as an example. While other companies sold the features and benefits of their products, Apple sold their *why*—challenging the status quo and thinking differently. And what happened? Apple won. They sold far more products than any of their competitors.

In the context of the nonprofit world, the product you're selling is your particular cause. Many charities tend to talk about *what* they do—their programs and the features of their programs—but they don't talk about *why* they do it. However, the truly successful charities tell stories to demonstrate why they exist. They tell stories on why their founders, president, and staff do what they do. They demonstrate that their work is not just a job or a way to raise money; it's a life mission.

In the book *Talk Like TED*, author Carmine Gallo recounts helping a bank executive prepare a presentation about his bank's involvement with United Way. The executive had crafted a dry story about the bank's commitment to the cause and how much his employees contributed each year, a presentation that was riddled with numbers and charts. It was informative, but not emotional. Then Gallo told the executive, "Tell me about your personal connection to United Way."

Instantly the executive forgot about his numbers and charts and dove into his story:

> I was two years old when my father abandoned the entire family. I was four years old when my mom remarried, and that's when I learned the definition of abuse. My first vivid memory was my mother lying in a pile of glass and my stepfather standing over her threatening to cut her throat if she didn't do exactly what he said. I remember thinking, where is my father and why is he allowing this man to do this to us?

The executive grew up to be an angry young man, until at twenty-five he enrolled in a United Way program that helped him curb his anger and make good choices. "I'm proud of the man I've become," he concluded.

Gallo encouraged the executive to scrap his original presentation and go with the personal account. The executive did, and ended up delivering a story that moved his audience to tears and brought forth a standing ovation. When he shared it with his co-workers, they gave the largest employee contribution of any division within his bank.[2]

Too often I find nonprofits are quick to jump into what they do, but they neglect this pivotal issue of the *why*. Without the *why*, it's just more flies buzzing in the room.

Remember Your Hero

Donald Miller's StoryBrand Marketing teaches that there are seven elements to a great story. The first element is that every great story has to have a hero—a main character.

In the context of nonprofit fundraising, the problem with our storytelling is that the nonprofit is the hero. It's all about us. It's all about the great things we are doing. It's all about our great victories. It's all about the people we are saving, rescuing, feeding, clothing, counseling, mentoring, and teaching. But all of this overlooks this fundamental principle:

The donor is the hero.

The donor is the main character. Every story we tell should be cast in light of our main character. What do they want? What are they grappling with? What fears do they have? We cannot assume that all the great things our organization is doing will matter one bit to them. In essence, we need to frame our storytelling with this question: "Why should they care?" Or "Why will it matter to them personally?"

As Donald Miller teaches, your relationship to the hero (the donor) should be that of the guide. In terms of movies, you are the Yoda to young Luke Skywalker. In *Rocky*, you are Mickey, the boxing coach for Rocky. In *The Hunger Games,* you are Haymitch for a troubled Katniss Everdeen. When your nonprofit organization understands what is bothering the donor and can guide them to a solution, you will in turn find a loyal donor.

I remember working with a family who was used to giving large sums of money each year. Frankly, to them I was just one more organization to stand in line for their money. However, as the conversation progressed, it became clear that they were dealing with succession issues in their family. When I pointed them to a solution for succession, the entire conversation changed. I was no longer an organization looking for a handout, but a trusted partner.

Once you've been able to establish your big *why* and who the hero of the story is, you can actually begin to craft real story.

Cutting Through the Noise with Great Story

What makes the difference between a run-of-the-mill story and a compelling story? In the book *Made to Stick*, brothers Chip and Dan Heath explore aspects of capturing an audience's attention, and these ideas can be applied to storytelling in fundraising.

The first way to capture attention is to create suspense, a "gap" in knowledge.[3] In other words, make donors feel like you know something they don't. In order to get someone to read beyond the subject line of your email or the tagline on your envelope, give them a teaser. For example, I received a newsletter for a homeless shelter. All the outer envelope said was, "With flip-flops on, Sally arrived at our door in the dead of winter." Instantly, this statement brought up questions that demanded answers. Who was Sally? Why was she at their door? Why was she wearing flip-flops in the dead of winter? Though I had no intention of donating, I had to open the letter to find out. (Turns out that Sally had been released from jail at four o'clock that morning and flip-flops were all she owned when she arrived at the homeless shelter's doorstep … in case you were wondering.)

Think of this need to satisfy curiosity as the "lame movie phenomenon." How many times have you suffered through a low quality film simply because you had to find out the ending? There's something in us that needs to fill in a knowledge gap.

As a fundraiser, use this innate human desire to grab a donor's attention. Create questions.

Creating questions also works on a larger scale to help donors own your vision as their own. As a fundraiser, your goal is to get them to start asking their own questions. Invite them to imagine with you, "What would happen if no one met this need?" Many nonprofits are good at explaining how donors' gifts can help, but they're not as good at getting donors to imagine what would happen if they didn't help. By prompting questions, you invite your donors to imagine how their gifts can make a difference.

Be Memorable

A great story that cuts through the noise must be memorable. When it's memorable, it allows a donor to retell it. What makes a story memorable?

Chip and Dan Heath spent years studying why some ideas catch on, and others flop. They came up with a simple acronym for sticky ideas: Simple, Unexpected, Concrete, Credible, Emotional, Story (SUCCESs). They claimed that if any idea contained these six elements, people would remember it.[4] Practically speaking, how do we accomplish each one of these aspects?

Simple—Your message has to be simple. The nonprofit Nothing But Nets does an excellent job of simplifying their message. Their mantra, "Send a net. Save a life," is so simple that it's unforgettable. Their goal is to stomp out malaria, a leading cause of death for children in Africa. They do so by providing insecticide-treated bed nets that protect children from mosquitoes, the main carriers of malaria. Because they have only one focus, providing nets, donors can easily remember their purpose.

Unexpected—People are more likely to remember something if it surprises them. In my earlier example of the envelope teaser, if the homeless shelter had told a story that started out, "With boots on, Sally walked up to our door in the dead of winter," I would have instantly tossed this envelope into the trash. But when the scenario became unexpected—the boots became flip-flops—the story transformed into something memorable.

Concrete—People remember what's tangible. If Nothing But Nets changed their slogan from "Send a Net. Save a life," to something less concrete like "Donate to eradicate a deadly disease," this phrase would still describe what they were doing, but it wouldn't be memorable. It would have no concrete images for us to connect the ideas to. However, we can picture one net, and to this mental picture we can tack on the idea of saving one life.

Credible—Your story has to be trustworthy. One way to create credibility is by being vulnerable. In general, people become suspicious of you when they know you have ulterior motives (especially if you're trying to get their money). Being open about your mistakes will help them realize that your nonprofit is honest. Don't limit your stories to only telling about the successes. People want to hear about your failure and your struggles too. Being vulnerable might mean sharing false assumptions that you had as you started your last project, or even as you started your organization. Tell how you discovered those assumptions were false and what you learned along the way. As you honestly share about the mistakes you've made, people will identify. They need to know that your ministry is still learning lessons, still getting better.

Emotional—Successful organizations realize that their stories must capture the emotion of their work. Stories have power to inspire feeling, connection, and action. Cara Jones, the Emmy Award-winning reporter and founder of Storytellers for Good, gives advice for choosing which stories to share: "Think about the ones that give your heart that little zingy feeling, bring a tear to your eye, or make you laugh."[5]

When your story captures emotion and resonates with its audience, donors will share it with others because they'll be sharing a part of themselves.

Focus on One

Telling a story, instead of giving information, ensures that you keep your donor focused on one person, or one plotline. In *Made to Stick*, the Heath brothers tell of researchers at Carnegie Mellon University who tested how people reacted to an abstract cause versus to the story of a single person. The researchers conducted a survey and offered to pay each participant five dollars. (The survey was irrelevant; it simply guaranteed each person had cash in hand.) After the survey, they gave participants an option to donate to Save the Children. Half of the participants received a request letter that gave an abstract summary of problems children in Africa faced, such as "Food shortages in Malawi are affecting more than three million children," and "Four million Angolans—one third of the population—have been forced to flee their homes."

The other half received a request letter about a single girl. The letter started out saying, "Any money that you donate will go to Rokia, a seven-year-old girl from Mali, Africa." The letter went on to describe Rokia's dire situation and how she would be helped by Save the Children if they donated. On average, participants who received the abstract statistics gave $1.14 and participants who received the letter about Rokia gave $2.38, over twice as much.[6]

As Mother Teresa once said, "If I look at the mass, I will never act. If I look at the one, I will." In order to move a story from being simply entertaining to moving someone to action, it has to be focused on one person. Stay away from big picture summaries, and instead, focus in on one person.

Connect the Story to the Impact

Several months ago I sat with a ministry leader who was quite the storyteller. I loved hearing his tales from another country about the people he met and the struggles he won. But at the end of the meeting, I didn't make a gift to his ministry because his stories didn't relate to his ministry's impact. They were colorful but didn't tie to the gift, like a movie with no theme.

Keep in mind the ROI concept of Chapter Six. No matter how vivid and moving your stories are, if they don't tie in to how your nonprofit is making a difference, they're not worth telling.

Share through Video

The importance of video cannot be overstated. We are a video generation. YouTube has billions of views per day and three hundred hours of video uploaded per minute.[7] Language, location and time are no longer barriers to fundraising. Your ministry can harness the power of video storytelling to reach a worldwide audience, anytime and anywhere.

Plus, posting a creative story requires minimal investment in equipment and no advanced filmmaking expertise. Just click on a few videos on YouTube and you'll see that their overall tone is direct, raw and somewhat edgy. In fact, if you use a highly polished, professional video, then potential donors might wonder why you spent so much money on production instead of on your area of service. However, raw doesn't mean slipshod. Know the point you are trying to accomplish.

The Promise of a Good Story

When I was practicing law, I found myself having to write briefs for the court. These "briefs" were massive fifty-page documents full of citations. I worked with a skilled senior partner who taught me his tedious craft. We literally would write and rewrite a paragraph nine different times until we got the message right.

Our care and planning meant that sometimes we saw the court adopt entire portions of our brief into their final opinions. Stated differently, the court was following the storyline that we laid out for them. In fact, one time I had a judge ask me to send my electronic copy of my brief so he could just edit it for his opinion.

The best ministries, the ones who are winning, are the ones who are continuing to refine their message. They refine their story. They readjust their message. They track their impact to see how their listening audience is responding.

Donors are like those judges. They are listening to see what they believe. What they believe, they adopt. What they adopt, they share. What they share with others will cut through the noise, because good story—like great movies—always wins.

* * *

CHAPTER EIGHT

Questions

1. How would you describe your organization's "why" to a potential donor in one minute or less?

2. On a scale of one to ten, how would you rank your organization's use of storytelling as a fundraising tool?

3. How can you take the donations you're receiving currently and start making revenue for your organization?

4. If you were to start using video on your website tomorrow, what is the first story you would tell? How would you make it memorable?

My Action Steps:

_____

_____

_____

_____

_____

_____

_____

_____

TREND NINE

The Increase of Legislative Scrutiny

"It is imperative that Congress make no changes to the charitable deduction that threatens the ability of nonprofit organizations to serve those most in need ... "
NATIONAL COUNCIL OF NONPROFITS

I've always thought charity was a good idea. Doing good and being generous make our world better.

But not everyone thinks so. Many lawmakers in this country are trending toward limiting, or even eliminating, charitable deductions. They make charity out to be the bad guy, when in truth, all they want is more money for government programs.

The real danger lies in the charitable world's ignorance of the threat it faces. In fact, nonprofits often live with the notion that they are too big to fail.

Lehman Brothers thought the same. In 1850, three Lehman Brothers founded their own dry goods store. They accepted cotton as payment, which ultimately led to trading cotton. Within a few years, trading commodities became the main focus of their business. They eventually established offices in New York, and over the years, their business changed with the times.

By 2008, Lehman Brothers had over $275 billion in assets and stood as the fourth largest investment firm in the country behind only household names like Goldman Sachs, Morgan Stanley, and Merrill Lynch. Their business and their name were a recognized part of the financial world. But like so many others, Lehman Brothers were heavily invested in sub-prime mortgages. After a series of drastic losses which spun out of control, Lehman Brothers filed for bankruptcy on September 15, 2008—the largest filing in United States history. Everyone thought they were too big to fail.

A Brief History of the Charitable Deduction

Charity, or charitable giving, has always existed. But it has not always had a charitable deduction associated with it.

In this country, charitable deductions first arose during World War I. The War Revenue Act of 1917 ruled that contributions to charitable organizations would be deductible (up to 15 percent of a person's taxable net income) so long as that person didn't receive any personal benefit from the contributions.

The deduction came about because the war was taking its toll on nonprofits, specifically educational institutions. They worried that their income would soon disappear. These institutions were faced with a double whammy. First, because of the war, their wealthiest donors had to pay increased war taxes. More taxes meant less giving. And second, their student population was dropping as young men headed off to war, which meant a drop in tuition income. Sen. Henry French Hollis explained:

> Usually people contribute to charities and educational objects out of their surplus. After they have done everything else they want to do, after they have educated their children and traveled and spent their money on everything they really want or think they want, then, if they have something left over, they will contribute it to a college or to the Red Cross or for some scientific purposes. Now, when war comes . . . that will be the first place where wealthy men will be tempted to economize, namely in donations to charity.[1]

The reasons the deduction was needed in 1917 are still the same reasons we need it today. When faced with rising taxes that eat away at disposable income, we want and need to encourage charity. And frankly, from the start, everyone acknowledged that government needed to provide this incentive particularly to the wealthy. Even in 1917, the *Washington Post* strenuously argued: "This country cannot abandon or impoverish the great structure of private charity and education that has been one of the most notable achievements of American civilization." [2]

The charitable deduction has continued to this day. It is one of the longest standing deductions in the history of the tax code. In fact, it is safe to say that for the past one hundred years it has been an accepted fact of American public life.

The Changing Landscape

Similar to the assumption the Lehman Brothers made, no one can assume that the charitable deduction will last forever. It must be defended if it is to be maintained. New threats to the deduction have surfaced. Several factors have arisen that have produced these threats.

One key factor has been the growth of the charitable world itself. The charitable world represents a key component of US GDP. As the number of charities has increased, there has been an increasing jealousy for providing certain organizations with a charitable benefit. For instance, some have argued that hospitals should not be provided tax exempt status and should be allowed to compete against for-profit medical providers. (In truth, that argument has carried little weight as evidenced by the shrinking number of nonprofit health care providers.)

A second key factor is the simple fact that some bad apples make the rest look bad. As the number of nonprofits has increased, so has the number of people who seek to use tax exempt status as a haven for bad activity. Unfortunately, there have been stories of church leaders and nonprofit leaders who used charitable dollars for their own benefit. With this misuse, people don't want to keep rewarding corrupt charities with tax benefits.

A third key factor is the assumption that the charitable deduction is designed to benefit the wealthy, and the wealthy shouldn't benefit in that way. People frame capping the deduction as a way to make the rich pay their fair share. But that argument that the wealthy shouldn't benefit from deductions undercuts the historical reality in which the deduction law was first passed. Since 1917, our country has sought to provide an incentive, even to the wealthy, for charitable giving. Indeed, the deduction was passed to encourage charitable donations from the wealthy. As a whole, we want to encourage that policy. We want charitable giving into our communities to continue. In an era where tax rates for individuals and businesses continue to rise at every sector, the deduction continues to provide incentive.

But these factors are not the driving force. It's about the government having more cash. As the federal deficit has spiraled, the government has started looking for new ways to create revenue. As they look, the charitable deduction pool—in excess of $300 billion dollars annually—appears tempting. Thus, the government has increasingly tried eliminating or capping charitable deductions.

Beginning with President Obama, we've seen proposals to limit the charitable deduction. Although his proposals were never passed, future presidents and legislators will likely offer similar proposals. As long as the government maintains its deficits and its hunger for revenue, the charitable deduction will remain a target. Ten years ago, few would have taken seriously the suggestion of eliminating the charitable deduction, but today's nonprofits need to be aware of this trend.

The Impact of Limiting the Charitable Deduction

The charitable deduction provides a vital incentive for donating to nonprofits. Researchers at Indiana University estimate that a change in the charitable deduction laws will drop charitable giving by between $5 billion and $13 billion.[3]

Taking away the deduction or reducing it will bring severe ripple effects. In another survey by Indiana University, two-thirds of high net worth donors said they would decrease their giving if they did not receive a deduction for donations.[4] Imagine what would happen if two-thirds of high net worth donors decreased their giving.

Dan Busby, president of the Evangelical Council for Financial Accountability, says that if the tax laws are more restrictive, fewer people will itemize deductions. Instead, they'll use a standard deduction, making it less appealing for smaller, low-income givers to donate to charity. Also, restrictions on property gifts could lower the amount of donated real estate—some of the largest gifts that nonprofits receive.[5]

In a world of changing demographics and an uncertain economy, nonprofits are already struggling to survive. Limiting deductions would bring unintended consequences. As our society ages, we'll need more and more help from nonprofits to care for the elderly, but those nonprofits will have less income if deductions are limited. Alternatively, if nonprofits do not fill this service need, then government programs will have to fill the need.

Those in favor of limiting the charitable deduction argue that it won't affect giving because donors give for reasons other than tax breaks. However, any nonprofit that has watched its income spike in December knows that tax deductions are a real incentive. Of all donations made to charity each year, 30 percent of those gifts typically come in December, and 10 percent come in the last two days of the year, December 30 and 31.[6] Without fail, giving peaks every year just before the tax cutoff date.

At the center of this debate lies a central question: Will restricting the charitable deduction actually solve anything? Slicing away at select deductions does nothing to address the fundamental question. Until the federal government reduces its spending, reducing the charitable deduction is at best a Band-Aid. It does nothing to solve the problem.

Our nation's national debt is at $20 trillion, and growing every day.[7] As a matter of basic discipline (or lack thereof), from 1900 to 2015 the United States overspent its income in 89 out of 115 years.[8] (Note, the charitable deduction has been present for 98 of those years.) The remedy is simple: spend less than you make. That is the systemic issue at hand. Unless and until future presidents and future congressional leaders decide to hold the line on spending, the effort to restrict a single line item like charitable deductions is futile. To put it differently, the charitable deduction is worth only $400 billion of annual giving at present. Hoping that $400 billion will affect a $20 trillion debt is like using a bathtub stopper to plug the Pacific Ocean. It won't work.

The Heart of the Matter

The central issue surrounding the charitable deduction is not eliminating tax benefits for the wealthy. To the contrary, the real issue is how much our society values charity. As a country, in 1917, our lawmakers made a statement that they wanted to encourage charity—not penalize it. Throughout the world, America is known for its charity. In times of crisis or calamity, people have looked to America to provide aid and relief, and we have responded. At a domestic level, the United States is known for the strength of its charitable organizations that provide everything from afterschool education to care for addicts and the elderly.

There are some who might contend that perhaps the government is the best director of all charity, and thus perhaps it is the government who should provide the care and services currently being provided by our nation's nonprofits. However, even a cursory glance at this supposition fails.

In a paper titled "Private Charity vs. Government Entitlements," David Longstreet points out that the government spends seventy cents of every dollar on administration for government entitlement programs. On the other hand, Longstreet notes that groups like Charity Navigator tell us that private charities spend, on average, just 10 percent of their budget on administration. Even if fundraising costs of 8 percent are added to the mix, private charities still only spend 18 percent on overhead. If Charity Navigator were evaluating government programs for fiscal effectiveness under its five-star rating system, those programs would receive zero stars. [9]

Few donors would be willing to give to an organization that spends 70 percent of its funding on itself. Private charities who are able to direct 82 percent of donated dollars to recipients are by far the better choice. [10]

In a Forbes article, Howard Husock argues that government social programs have their place as does private charity. No one, for instance, would think that private charity could replicate social security. However, regarding private charity, he states, "Here, in other words, is where government cannot replace charity—when the need is for committed, idealistic staff (paid or volunteer) to work with individuals on specific problems." Husock uses the example of job training. The government program, Workforce Investment Act, found jobs for 56 percent of its people, of which 20 percent lost their newly acquired jobs. In contrast, Cincinnati Works, a privately funded charity led by Dave and Lianne Phillips, focuses upon instilling proper job habits and attitudes. What is their job placement and retention rate? A whopping 84 percent.[11]

The nonprofit world represents the very spirit upon which this country was founded—innovation, passion, and freedom. Today, all across our nation, we have individuals passionate about their causes. They invest countless hours, go without sleep, and wake up every day with new ideas about how they can serve people and make our world better. Surely, we want to continue to encourage that activity instead of letting that energy and passion get caught in the throes of government bureaucracy. (And anyone who has ever stood in a Department of Motor Vehicles line waiting for action knows what I'm talking about.) Husock punctuates his article by saying, "[I]t is, similarly, high time for liberals to acknowledge the failure of government to (successfully) replace what charitably-funded, non-governmental programs do best: help individuals thrive."[12]

Take Action

For a long time, the charitable deduction has largely gone undisturbed. But now, in the midst of rising government debt and the call for revenue, that deduction is being called into question. The nonprofit world, like Lehman Brothers, must not assume they are too big to fail. The charitable deduction is not a permanent right.

As a nonprofit leader, you can prepare for this trend by communicating your value to those outside your organization. Dan Busby encourages nonprofits to share the value of their work to a broader sphere. Internally, most nonprofits have highly dedicated staff members who wholeheartedly believe in the value of their work. And most nonprofits communicate this value to their donors through emails, newsletters, Facebook posts and web articles. But what about those outside of your organization? Do they know how much of an impact you're making? Does your city council know what you offer to the community? Are you known statewide, nationwide, or even worldwide for the important role you fill?

Speak up about your nonprofit, and about the value of charity as a whole. As opportunities arise to join lobbying efforts for the charitable deduction, don't merely assume that others will take up the fight. Join the local nonprofit association group. Join an industry trade group. Write the occasional letter to your senator or congressman. Moreover, get involved in what your community cares about. Attend your city council meetings. Get involved in local politics. Send press releases to your local media informing them about unique ways you serve the community. Be creative, but whatever you do, make sure people outside of your organization know your charity's value. You can't live in a cocoon. It stands to reason that the more the community knows about your service, the more they'll work to protect that service.[13]

Edmund Burke once said, "All that is necessary for the triumph of evil is for good men to do nothing." The passionate and effective work of the nonprofit world must be preserved. Don't let a debt-laden government choose temporary solutions for cash over the long-term good of our communities.

* * *

CHAPTER NINE

Questions

1. Have you communicated your nonprofit's value to spheres outside of your organization?

2. What are the major areas of service you provide, and how do you do a better job at these than the government could?

3. What are measurable ways you can demonstrate your organization's impact?

4. Is your nonprofit actively talking to local leaders and representatives about charitable tax deductions?

My Action Steps:

_____

_____

_____

_____

_____

_____

_____

_____

TREND TEN

The Rise of Giving Influencers

"Never underestimate the influence you have on others."
LAURIE BUCHANAN

I once had a meeting worth $15 million. Let me explain. I was discussing an estate plan with a client and his wife. They'd already decided how much they wanted to leave to their children; everything else they wanted to go to charity. They simply didn't realize what their plan provided. As I walked them through the estate plan, I quickly showed them that after they'd given money to their kids and paid substantial estate taxes, there would still be millions left for charity. Why wait until they died to give it away?

Immediately after the meeting ended, they called their attorney and asked for a revised estate plan. In one swoop, charity picked up $15 million dollars. All because of a giving influencer.

Who are Giving Influencers?

Giving influencers are those who hold sway over others' giving. Typically giving influencers fall into four categories: financial advisors, community foundation leaders, philanthropic advisors, and peer influencers. (For the purposes of this chapter, peer influencers will not be addressed because they have essentially been discussed in our chapter on major donors.)

These giving influencers have risen to greater standing because of the increased number of charitable organizations. As more and more nonprofit organizations spring up, it becomes increasingly difficult for donors to decide where to give. Just recently, I sat with a friend who told me one of the biggest burdens that his client faced was the decision on where to give.

Giving influencers have increased as the level of wealth rises. Because people have grown wealth in excess of what they need and what their children need, some of the wealthy are now looking to charity as a place to make contributions. But they need people to guide their giving. The nonprofit world should understand this trend toward giving influencers. Each influencer has a role of guiding charitable donations, whether through financial acumen, life coaching, knowledge of charitable organizations, or relational capital.

The Rise of Financial Advisors

As wealth transferring has increased, financial advisors have increased in importance. As a career, financial planning is expected to grow 30 percent through the year 2024.[1] One hundred years ago only, an elite few families in America had wealth, such as the Carnegies or Rockefellers. This group had the money and had a lot of it. The rest of America only dreamed of what it would be like to live in wealth.

Now, a hundred years later, wealth has grown dramatically. According to CNBC, in 2014 the US gained nearly 500,000 new millionaires—raising the overall millionaire total to 10.1 million. With this rate of growth, there are now more than twice the number of millionaire households than there were in 1996.[2] In the past twenty years, the millionaires have doubled. No longer just a few, the elite are now a numerous force. Along with this increase of wealth has come the increased need for financial advisors to guide them.

As the War and Boomer generations age and prepare to pass on their wealth, they're asking, "What do we do with all this money?" They've spent a lifetime accumulating wealth, and now that it's time to pass it on, they're unsure where it should go. Essentially, when deciding who to leave their wealth to, each person has three options: Their wealth will either go to their kids, to the government, or to charity. Naturally, most people want to leave the majority of their wealth to their children, the traditional heirs, but they're realizing more and more that this may not be the best idea. The Boomer generation is filled with second or third marriages and blended families. In many families, the kids have become skeptical of their parents, and the parents have become skeptical of their kids. Parents don't always want to entrust their hard-earned wealth to children who don't share their values.

Also, there's the question of how much wealth is beneficial for kids to inherit. Parents want to prepare their kids for the future, not ruin their future. Leaving millions of dollars to their children might ruin them, especially if the kids aren't ready to receive it. Unprepared to handle a large sum of money, the kids will most likely misuse it, and the money may even ruin them altogether. Even if the kids survive this inundation of wealth, history shows that the family wealth won't survive. Statistically, most inherited family wealth doesn't survive past one hundred years. Ninety percent of assets are depleted by the third generation. The parent earns it, the child inherits it, and the grandchild squanders it. So Boomers are wondering both what to do with their wealth and how to make it last for future generations.

The Role of Financial Advisors

Enter the financial advisor. With so much wealth being passed on and so many families in turmoil, many financial advisors are now specializing in legacy planning, teaching families how to use strategies for dealing with wealth. This is especially true of the Boomer generation. According to Jerry Nuerge, owner and founder of the Financial Independence Group, "The Baby Boomer generation truly looks for advocates, professionals that will step in their shoes, see the world as they see it and relate and counsel them."[3] Members of the Boomer generation want help as they near retirement and start thinking about what legacy they will leave their families.

Financial advisors are also gaining popularity within the world of charity. *The 2014 U.S. Trust Study of High Net Worth Philanthropy* showed that among high net worth households that donated to a nonprofit, 45 percent of them consulted with an advisor before donating.[4] Before high net worth donors gave, almost half of them talked with their financial advisor to decide how much to give. According to the World Wealth Report, there is a growing desire among donors to ensure that their giving is actually making a difference. This desire has led them to seek just as much professional advice in donating to charities as in making financial investments.[5] From these statistics, we can see that financial advisors are a growing trend that can't be ignored.

These advisors aren't just attorneys drafting up a will or a trust. They play a crucial role in helping a family make value decisions such as planning their legacy and discussing how much to keep for their kids, how much to save for their retirement, and how much to pass on to charity.

"The advisors are in a position where they can encourage individuals to make gifts and to make more gifts," says Michael King, vice president of Gift Planning Services at the National Christian Foundation. "They understand the family's full financial picture, how much they want to pass on to kids and how much they'll have left over to give to charity."[6] Of donors who work with a financial advisor, 35 percent of them say the advisor has helped them give more.[7]

Ron Blue started Kingdom Advisors as a coalition of Christian financial advisors back in 2003 with just sixteen advisors. More than ten years later, it has grown to 2,200 advisors. He speaks of the influence financial advisors have over their clients: "When an advisor looks into somebody's financial situation, they see their values, their goals, their priorities—they see their heart."[8] Marty Bicknell, CEO of Mariner Wealth Advisors, one of the top independent financial planning firms in the country says, "A good advisor knows what a client's philanthropic goals are and the potential tax benefits associated with donations. A great advisor understands why the client has the desire to support a specific cause and the emotional impact that cause has on them or their loved ones."[9] As financial advisors step into this role of trusted counselor, their advice influences a person's finances more than almost anyone else. With financial advisors' increased influence, they hold sway over clients' financial strategy, estate planning, and charitable giving.

Charities and Financial Advisors

With this surplus of financial advisors, a clear trend has emerged: charities developing strategic relationships with financial advisors to grow their fundraising efforts. A single financial advisor may have three hundred or more clients. Some of those clients will be charitably inclined. Thus, relationships with five to ten financial advisors may effectively grow your reach by three thousand people.

However, it's critical to realize that you cannot simply go to a financial advisor and ask them to provide you with names of donors. The ideal relationship with a financial advisor is a partnership. There may be current donors associated with your organization who could benefit from enhanced financial planning. In other words, your nonprofit could become a referral source for key advisors. As an advisor sees that you're not simply mining for potential donors, they're more likely to start recommending your nonprofit for clients' donations.

The Birth of Community Foundations

As wealth has grown, so have community foundations. Generally speaking, community foundations are donor-advised-fund organizations. At a community foundation, a donor can set up a charitable account, make a contribution, receive an immediate tax deduction, and then make gifts from the account to charities they want to support.

The first community foundation, the Cleveland Foundation, was established in 1914. Since that time, community foundations experienced generally steady growth. By the 1990s, as the stock market began experiencing a steady uptick, the donor-advised funds began experiencing more marked growth. In 1991, Fidelity established the first commercial donor-advised fund followed by Vanguard in 1997 and Schwab Charitable in 1999.

From 2010 to 2014, the donor-advised fund world experienced even greater acceleration. To illustrate, in 2010 donor-advised funds received $9.35 billion; by 2014, that number had grown to $19.66 billion—an increase of almost 200 percent.[10]

Donor-advised funds have grown because of their simplicity. A donor-advised fund is easy—most allow for setup online, and for gifts to charities to be completed online. Donor-advised funds allow donors to do all their giving through their account (to church, missions, schools, etc.) and receive one tax receipt at year end. Donors may also contribute appreciated assets like publicly traded securities and even closely held assets.

It used to be that donors would set up private foundations for their giving. But private foundations require administration and a tax return filed every year. Those tax returns are publicly available information. Thus, private foundations are not truly private. On the other hand, giving through donor-advised funds can be done anonymously. For these reasons, community foundations have become a preferred method of giving.

Community Foundations as Giving Influencers

As donor-advised funds have grown in prominence, so have community foundation leaders' influence on giving. Community foundation leaders know their donors. Similarly, because these leaders send grants out to so many organizations, they tend to be familiar with nonprofits in their community and beyond. At The Signatry, our donors have made grants to thousands of nonprofits. However, the nonprofits may not always know who these grants came from because of the donors' ability to make anonymous gifts through their donor-advised funds.

Like financial advisors, a community foundation leader might work with hundreds of donors. Their engagement with those donors is often at a personal, advisory level. Those donors want to know how to make an impact in the community. I remember working with one donor who only wanted to open an account for convenience. However, as we worked together, he appreciated our friendship. We had lunches and dinners together. We talked a lot about family, and about his dreams. He shared his desire to impact orphans and international mission efforts. As time went on, he trusted that I knew his desires and wishes. Ultimately, he made a large gift to his fund and asked our foundation to be responsible for making gifts in accordance with his wishes.

Working with Community Foundations

As with financial advisors, don't expect to show up on the doorstep of a community foundation and ask for names of potential donors. Early in my career, I had an organization's president call and leave me a voicemail, which went something like this:

> My name is Joe Nonprofit Leader, and I'd like you to come out and visit our event. I think you'll see that we are the answer to so many of your donor's needs—they are looking for a great place to give, and we are that place.

I didn't call him back.

As with any key relationship, it is essential to get to know the community foundation leader and learn what objectives they are trying to accomplish and how your organization might be a contributor. Joe Nonprofit should have asked if he could meet with me to find out our foundation's goals and how we serve our donors.

Like a financial advisor, many community foundation leaders work with donors on a gift-planning basis to help them accomplish their charitable objectives. In a similar way, nonprofit organizations may introduce some of their donors to the community foundation to help them accomplish their charitable objectives.

On the other hand, as your organization grows in relationship with a community foundation leader, there may be an opportunity where you'll be introduced to donors of that community foundation—people that you may not have had any chance to meet. Whether financial advisor or community foundation leader, it is essential to build a relationship of trust and mutual benefit.

Philanthropic Advisors

In a similar vein to financial advisors and community foundations, there is a growing field of philanthropic advisors. This field is still new and relatively immature. But more and more, people serious about their charitable giving are hiring consultants for help.

That consultant may look like the following:

Due Diligence on Causes or Organizations: Some consultants function as investment advisors on behalf of clients. They research particular segments of the nonprofit world. They may also research specific organizations and determine effectiveness. They'll prepare reports for the donor that actually look like investment summaries.

Program Manager: These consultants will run a donor's granting program. They'll monitor which grants to send out, track how the funds are used, and report the results each grant achieved. Some consultants will design a giving program to achieve maximum impact on how funds will be used.

Giving Plan Design: Some consultants work with donors or donor families to help design a charitable giving plan. Part of that plan is to draw out a family's mission, vision and values, and then to design that plan in accordance with those values.

Mediation: More rarely, a few consultants will work with donors when their grants or grant purposes go awry. For example, if the donor gave to a specific project and the nonprofit later needed to divert the funds to another purpose, the consultant would step in to mediate the dispute.

In addition to these types of consultants, there are now different types of organizations that provide varying levels of accountability or transparency on the operations of an organization. These include groups like Charity Navigator, Evangelical Council for Financial Accountability, or Guidestar.

Philanthropic advisors generally look for nonprofits that serve a particular sector or meet a particular need a donor is trying to address. However, they also look for the most effective nonprofits with the ability to learn and learn fast. Your nonprofit organization must be prepared to demonstrate its efficiency and effectiveness. Showing up on the radar of these kinds of philanthropic advisors can propel your organization into new levels of growth.

You won't just discover donors by meeting donors. You'll discover donors through their gatekeepers. Those gatekeepers are financial advisors, community foundation leaders, and philanthropic advisors. Make sure you are developing relationships with those gatekeepers—relationships of mutual benefit. Similarly, recognize that philanthropic advisors do in fact exist and that they are looking for efficient and effective organizations. Let that be incentive to improve your own organization's systems and efficiencies.

* * *

CHAPTER TEN

Questions

1. Have you held back from working with giving influencers? What's been keeping you from doing so?

2. What are some ways you can network with giving influencers in your area?

3. What is your organization's next step for broadening your sphere of influence among advisors?

My Action Steps:

_____

_____

_____

_____

_____

_____

_____

_____

_____

_____

BRINGING IT ALL TOGETHER

It's about Generosity—Not Transactions

"No earthly investment pays so large an interest as charity."
JOSEPH COOK

Giving is changing from transactions to generosity.

Let me explain. I have a friend who has been a fundraiser for a long time. She describes part of her early experience chasing donors. One man was particularly difficult to catch. He knew the drill, and he always managed to avoid her call or her visit.

But one day they happened to be attending the same luncheon. Determined not to lose her opportunity, she approached him with boldness and asked whether he'd be part of their current campaign. His curt reply caught her off guard: "How much?" Not to be outdone, she responded with similar brevity, "$250,000!"

She was proud of herself for such a big demand. He surprised her, however, when he asked her to turn around. She complied. He promptly pulled out his checkbook, propped it on her shoulder, and wrote out a check for $250,000. His parting comment to her was simply, "I thought you were going to make it hurt a lot more."

She walked away not sure whether to feel grateful or repulsed. She felt glad for his generosity—even shocked that he was ready to give such a large amount and would probably have given more had she asked for it. But she also felt dehumanized. She had been turned into an object, both literally as he used her for a desk to write out his check, and figuratively as he treated her like a nuisance to be dealt with. For him, the gift was merely a transaction.

This attitude is not what you want for your donors. You want them to move beyond transactions and into generosity. It's not about the gift; it's about the heart. Stated differently, it's about the idea that living generously is the best way of life.

Why is the idea of living generously so powerful? Living generously is transformational. It changes people. And when people become truly generous, they act without regard to deductions or appeals.

It is this change—toward helping people live generously—that will revolutionize the entire game.

Where We've Been—Transactional Giving

For a long time now, direct mail has been the king of fundraising. The theory has been to send out enough mail that only a small percentage needs to respond to make it worthwhile. Or in the context of the church, the plate gets passed and we drop in cash. Or we attend a banquet, an appeal is made, and we make a pledge or write out a check. The formula is pretty standard: make an appeal and get a check—transactional giving.

This form of giving does not typically require a deep emotional response. Need plus money equals transactional gift. I had a friend who complained about this form of giving. He told me about the many people who regularly approached him about supporting them monthly. He told them plainly, "I don't make payments; I like to make gifts." He wanted to be emotionally engaged, giving because he cared.

On the other hand, I met with a donor who was so used to getting appeals for monthly support that he had fully accepted this transactional method as the only way to give. In fact, he supported as many as twenty ministries on a monthly basis. When he met with me, he quickly assumed that I wanted monthly support. He told me to simply mail him a letter with an invoice, and he'd send me $200 per month! No emotional engagement. For him, the gift was a business transaction. But this old model is changing.

Generosity—The Big Idea

In the past several years, we've seen a growing body of what some refer to as the science of generosity. *The Paradox of Generosity* documents the work of a national study started in 2010. *American Generosity: Who Gives and Why* is the flagship volume of the Science of Generosity Initiative. These works reflect similar studies of varying degrees.

The sum of these studies is simply that generous people live happier, healthier, and more purposeful lives. But what does it mean to be generous? Smith and Davidson in *The Paradox of Generosity* define generosity as "the virtue of giving good things to others freely and abundantly." They also note the origin of the word was associated with nobility or nobility of spirit. To draw out the point further they state:

> Generosity ... is a learned character trait that involves both attitudes and actions—entailing as a virtue both a disposition to give liberally and an actual practice of giving liberally. Generosity is not a random idea or a haphazard behavior, but rather in its mature form at least a basic, personal, moral orientation to life.[1]

In short, generosity is a learned behavior. Once it is learned, it becomes a framework for everyday living. It becomes a way of life.

In contrast, giving which is transactional or event-oriented doesn't have the same emotional appeal. Accordingly, Smith and Davidson point out that things like blood donation, organ donation, estate giving and lending possessions don't develop the kind of regular sustained practice that leads to a change in behavior. However, "many practices can eventually become routines, and even sometimes mindless habits."[2]

The Power of a Generous Life

Frank is an elderly friend of mine. He lived a Forrest Gump type of life—a feather floating in the wind wherever opportunity took him. He went to school, joined the service and learned to fly an airplane. That eventually led to a prosperous job with the airlines. His kids got involved with a church, and in Frank's terms he got "hooked on Jesus." For more than thirty years, Frank was a regular tither, giving 10 percent of his income.

Eventually Frank started a business, and his tax liability started to grow. He looked for other options for giving more and stumbled upon the organization that later became The Signatry. Through The Signatry, he found he could give away not only his income, but also things like ownership interest in his business and real estate. Frank became radically generous and began giving far more than 10 percent. Today, he'll quietly tell you that giving has opened up his eyes to things he never would have seen. "Giving has changed my life," says Frank.

Or consider another friend of mine, Mike. Mike was a hard-driving business guy. He lived a hard and fast life. He quickly grew a business, and then lost it. He started over and grew a business again. But this time, Mike tried something different. He took some time off from work and visited an orphanage in Thailand.

While at the orphanage, his perspective on business changed. He realized that his wealth was not in his bank account but in the lives of the people he could impact. He started his own orphanage in Haiti and a ministry called the Global Orphan Project. Mike committed to using his own wealth to pay the operating overhead of the ministry so that all contributions could go directly to programs.

Mike's goal is to take his last breath at the same time he gives away his last dollar. He tells me that his advisors aren't too happy about that decision—they caution him to save a bit more. But Mike smiles and simply says, "There's freedom in generosity."

The Benefits of Generosity

Frank and Mike are just two examples of the many people I've known who have grown in their own generosity. Part of the key to their growth is that others invested in their respective journeys of generosity. Others were more concerned about Frank's and Mike's journeys than they were in getting a gift for their organization. In fact, groups like Generous Giving, Generous Church and The Signatry have risen up to coach people in how to become generous.

The power of making an investment in a person's generosity journey involves a paradigm shift. In the book *Coach Your Champions*, Eric Foley suggests that generosity is not inherent in us; it must be taught. Many nonprofits make the mistake of thinking, "If I just use the right platform, have the right wording or find the right timing, then I'll convince people to give." But Foley points out that if people don't have a lifestyle of generosity, no matter how effective your fundraising tactics are, they still won't give. You need to impart value to them, realizing they aren't just a means for you to reach your goal, but you have much to offer them.[3] We need to become more concerned about the interests of the donor instead of their potential to make a donation to our organization.

What are the benefits of being generous? How do donors benefit?

This seems like a contradiction, that the more we give, the more we gain. Yet as one proverb states, "A generous man will prosper; whoever refreshes others will be refreshed."[4] Living generously brings many benefits.

Better Health

The Paradox of Generosity cites multiple studies showing that generosity triggers chemical systems in the brain that lead to happiness. One of these chemicals is endorphin, a natural painkiller. The same chemical released from exercise (the "runner's high") or to numb physical pain is released when you give. Giving also releases serotonin, a chemical associated with better moods and less depression; oxytocin, associated with social bonding; and dopamine, which regulates rewards and learning and promotes prosocial behavior.

Conversely, the study showed that non-generous people have high amounts of cortisol, the body's stress hormone that, helpful in small spurts to deal with a crisis, can be detrimental to health over long periods of time.[5]

Plentiful Relationships

Generous people have a larger social network. Volunteering forces people to get out into their community and connect with people, and those who volunteer have a sense of belonging with the various churches, associations and charities they help.[6] People need each other. When they give, they connect with a community beyond themselves.

Sense of Personal Power

People who give believe they can make a difference. They don't just sit back and complain about everything wrong with the world; they decide to become the change they want to see in the world. This intentionality leads to a sense of personal power and the feeling that their lives matter—that they can make a difference. And generous people also have greater discipline in their lifestyle, recognizing that generosity often requires doing without something so that they have extra to give to someone in need.[7]

The Inexplicably Miraculous

Those who live generously tell story after story of times they decided to be generous, even when it didn't make sense, and they experienced an increase of wealth as a result. We're not suggesting you give in order to get, but generosity often has surprising results. For example, Dayton Moore, general manager of the Kansas City Royals baseball team, said, "Marianne and I became regular givers when we moved to Atlanta, and that's when my career began to take off."[8]

Rick Warren, pastor of Saddleback Church in California, recounts a similar story. When their church was buying a piece of land for $9 million, Rick and his wife Kay felt that they needed to donate two years' worth of his salary—$100,000—toward purchasing the land. They committed to this amount in front of his congregation, not knowing where the money would come from. The next week, Zondervan publishers called to offer him a book deal with a contract for $150,000, enough to cover the gift and provide that year's salary. [9]

How to Engage Donors in Generous Living

Encouraging donors to live generously is perhaps the most powerful trend in front of the nonprofit world. The nonprofit world is sitting upon the largest wealth transfer in the history of our country. We know two key facts about this transfer: first, people are thinking for the first time about making large and generous gifts. Second, a majority of people in this country still do not live generous lives and are reluctant to leave large gifts behind.[10] Stated plainly, if we help donors live generously, we'll be a gateway for an outpouring of generosity.

How do we help people live more generously?

The first step involves a paradigm shift in the nonprofit world. We have to resolve that what we want *for* donors— generous lives—is far more important than what we want *from* them— gifts for our organization.

A second key step is to realize that donors give to multiple organizations. They are not our donors. They are people on a journey. The implication behind these first two points means that we can point people to other organizations. We can help them find what is best for them—what fits their passion.

I was blown away to see how one ministry lived out these two steps with my daughter Jessica. My wife, Brooke, and I tried to instill generosity in our kids as we raised them. As a family, we had a donor-advised fund. From time to time we would have family meetings where each child recommended an organization to grant to from our fund. When my daughter Jessica was thirteen, she read a story about kids with disabilities and decided she wanted to find a ministry that helped these kids as well as evangelized to them. We searched and searched but could not find any ministry that fit her criteria. A couple months later, I had a meeting at McDonalds with a ministry leader. My assistant had scheduled the meeting for me, so when I met the guy, I asked him what he did.

"We minister to kids with disabilities," he said.

My jaw dropped. "Do you do evangelism?" I asked.

"Of course we do evangelism!" he answered. I nearly fell off my chair.

I told him about my daughter and how long we had searched unsuccessfully to find an organization that did exactly what he did. Now here's where he earned major brownie points: He lived in California, but made a special trip from California to Kansas City just to meet Jessica. He came to my house, met with her, and told her she was at the age where people get inspired for life, and that she should follow her passion. There was nothing in it for the ministry leader, but he had a bigger vision for his donors than what they could give. He cared about them as people.

A third key is to make sure that donors hear the stories of other givers on the journey of generosity. The goal is never to share how much someone gave, but rather to share the wrestling they endured in order to learn how to give. Generous Giving regularly hosts Journeys of Generosity events—twenty-four-hour events where donors get together to share their struggles with wealth. How much is enough? How much do we leave to our children? How much do we give away? Sometimes those stories can be shared at events and banquets, but the emphasis should always be on the journey and not the amount of the gift.

A fourth step is to seek engagement—going beyond writing a check. Attending Generous Giving events and hearing the stories of others influenced Frank's journey. He also became exposed to more and more organizations that showed him a bigger and broader world. Mike's journey was influenced by his visits to orphanages in different parts of the world. And the emphasis should be on the fact that it is a journey. Few people wake up and instantly become generous. It takes time and relationship.

A fifth key step is advocacy. Once donors progress in their own journeys, it's a powerful thing to have them share their stories with others. After I met Frank and began learning his story, I sought to take him with me on as many lunch appointments and small group meetings as I could. When he saw that his story could influence others, this reinforced his own journey. He became a generosity advocate.

Finally, perhaps the biggest step of all is to practice generosity in our own lives. As the classic proverb says, you don't want to be the plumber with leaky pipes. It's hard to teach generosity if you are not personally generous yourself. Every day I'm challenged by this thought.

I try to make a habit of generosity in the everyday—spending a little extra time at a restaurant talking with my server as he shares his life story, paying for the car behind me in a drive-through, making a fancy breakfast for my family on the weekend. Sometimes I joke with my kids that I've been so generous I've given away their college education.

I realized I must be doing something right in living out this generosity thing when one of my sons came to me and told me he was giving away a third of his summer income. He'd worked hard over the summer to afford to go to a summer program in Colorado and still have savings left over to get him through the school year. However, a college classmate of his at the same program had only sixty dollars left in his bank account and didn't know how he'd make it through the school year. So my son decided to give him a third of his money.

As a parent, my first response was, "Are you out of your mind? That's completely irresponsible! How are you going to get by?"

"I'm going to have to learn to live with less," he said. And then he quoted C.S. Lewis on me: "If your generosity doesn't curb your desires, it's probably not generous." Schooled by my own son. He gets it from his mother.

But it is a good thought. Generosity starts with us as the influencers, the ones encouraging others to give. I can think of no better way to influence our world than to live generously and to encourage others to do the same. Generous people make for generous communities and ultimately a better world. It is not just a trend, but an aspiration.

* * *

EPILOGUE

The Challenge to Change

If you're like me, you have lived through quite a few revolutions—the Sexual Revolution, the Jesus Revolution, the Reagan Revolution, the Technology Revolution . . . I could go on and on.

We are now undergoing another great revolution in history—the Generous Giving Revolution. And I am excited to work with churches, ministries and other nonprofits around the world to accomplish great things.

After nearly two decades of working with individual donors, I am convinced we have at least a twenty-year window for major donations. By acting now, we can help ensure that history's greatest transfer of wealth contributes to the causes so dear to us.

In the midst of the most exciting time in the history of charity, countless nonprofits are skating in circles, unaware of the changes taking place all around them.

But you're aware. You can be like Wayne Gretzky, and focus your efforts on where the puck is going in the fundraising world. Now lace up your boots and skate to it.

REFERENCES

Preface

1. Kenneth W. Gronbach, *The Age Curve* (New York: Amacom, 2008), xv-xvii.

Introduction

1. "Wayne Gretzky Quotes." accessed June 22, 2015, http://www.brainyquote.com/quotes/quotes/w/waynegretz383282.html.

2. Wayne Gretzky and Rick Reilly, *Gretzky: An Autobiography* (New York: HarperCollins, 1990).

3. Indiana University-Purdue University Indianapolis, *Giving USA 2017: Annual Report on Philanthropy for the Year 2016.* Indianapolis, Indiana University, 2016.

4. National Center for Nonprofit Statistics, The Nonprofit Almanac, 2012, http://nccsdataweb.urban.org/NCCS/extracts/nonprofitalmanacflyerpdf.pdf.

5. "Get Ready for $40 Trillion Transfer," *The Nonprofit Times,* last modified February 19, 2013, http://www.thenonprofittimes.com/news-articles/get-ready-for-40-trillion-transfer/.

Chapter 1

1. "Three Reasons Most Retiring Baby Boomer Business Owners Will Not Be Able to Sell Their Businesses," *Tennessee Valley Group, Inc.*, accessed July 9, 2015, http://tnvalleygroup.com/reasons-retiring-baby-boomer-business-owners-sell-business/.

2. Dave Bernard, "The Baby Boomer Number Game," *U.S. News & World Report*, March 23, 2012, http://money.usnews.com/money/blogs/on-retirement/2012/03/23/the-baby-boomer-number-game.

3. Chris Cox and Bill Archer, "Why $16 Trillion Only Hints at the True US Debt," *Wall Street Journal*, Nov. 28, 2012, http://www.wsj.com/articles/SB10001424127887323335320457812 7374039087636.

4. Karl Zinsmeister, "DoNation: Which Americans Give Most to Charity?" *Philanthropy Roundtable*, Summer 2013, http://www.philanthropyroundtable.org/topic/donor_intent/donation.

5. David E. Campbell, "It's Social Ties—Not Religion—That Makes the Faithful Give to Charity," *Time*, November 26, 2013, http://ideas.time.com/2013/11/26/religious-people-are-more-charitable/.

Chapter 2

1. Steve MacLaughlin, *Charitable Giving Report: How Nonprofit Fundraising Performed in 2016. Blackbaud*, last modified October 2017, https://institute.blackbaud.com/wp-content/uploads/2017/02/2016-Charitable-Giving-Report.pdf.

2. MacLaughlin, *Charitable Giving*.

3. Joanne Fritz, "Report Confirms Why Millennials Are Crucial to Future of Nonprofits," About.com, accessed June 23, 2015, http://nonprofit.about.com/od/generationalfundraising/a/Report-Confirms-Why-Millennials-Are-Crucial-To-Future-Of-Nonprofits.htm.

4. Achieve, *The 2013 Millennial Impact Report*, accessed June 23, 2015, http://casefoundation.org/wp-content/uploads/2014/11/MillennialImpactReport-2013.pdf.

5. Tami Heim, interview with the author, June 11, 2015.

6. "Recognising and Rewarding Online Advocacy," *Smart Insights*, last updated August 5, 2013, http://www.smartinsights.com/online-pr/online-pr-outreach/creating-and-maintaining-on-line-advocacy/.

7. Achieve, 2013 *Millennial Impact Report*.

8. Clara Shih, *The Facebook Era: Tapping Online Social Networks to Build Better Products, Reach New Audiences and Sell More Stuff* (Boston: Pearson Education, 2011).

9. Shea Bennett, "How Do People Spend Their Time Online?" *Social Times*, Last updated May 7, 2012, http://www.adweek.com/socialtimes/online-time/463670.

10. Andrew Lipsman, "Teens & Older Demos Driving Gains in U.S. Smartphone Penetration," *ComScore* (blog), May 8, 2015, http://www.comscore.com/Insights/Blog/Teens-Older-Demos-Driving-Gains-in-U.S.-Smartphone-Penetration.

11. Lisa Kiplinger, "Millennials LOVE Their Smartphones: Deal with It," *USA Today*, September 27, 2014, http://www.usatoday.com/story/money/personalfinance/2014/09/27/millennials-love-smartphones-mobile-study/16192777/.

12. "The Next Generation of American Giving," *Blackbaud*, accessed June 23, 2015, https://www.blackbaud.com/nonprofit-resources/generational-giving-report-infographic.

13. "Statistics," *Mobile Cause*, accessed August 19, 2015, https://www.mobilecause.com/statistics/#.

Chapter 3

1. Holly Hall, "An Alumnus Teaches a University How to Double Its Donations," *Chronicle of Philanthropy*, July 24, 2011, https://philanthropy.com/article/A-University-Doubles-Donations/158095.

2. Charles Duhigg, "How Companies Learn Your Secrets," *The New York Times Magazine,* February 16, 2012, http://www.nytimes.com/2012/02/19/magazine/shopping-habits.html?pagewanted=1&_r=2&hp.

3. Leigh Kessler, interview with the author, June 13, 2016.

4. "Creating Connections: An Epsilon Client Story," *Epsilon*, accessed June 21, 2016, http://www.epsilon.com/wp-content/uploads/2014/10/Save_the_children_CS.pdf.

5. Avi Wolfman-Arent, "Finding the Best Donors Through Data Cooperatives," *The Chronicle of Philanthropy*, February 27, 2015, https://philanthropy.com/article/Finding-the-Best-Donors/189909.

6. Wolfman-Arent, "Finding the Best Donors."

7. Don McNamara, "Getting Cooperation," *The NonProfit Times*, March 15, 2013, http://www.thenonprofittimes.com/news-articles/getting-cooperation/.

8. Nicole Wallace, "Nonprofits Find New Donors with Databases That Track Connections," *The Chronicle of*

Philanthropy, November 16, 2014, http://www.thenonprof-ittimes.com/news-articles/getting-cooperation/.

9. Matthew Frattura, interview with the author, June 24, 2016.

10. Wolfman-Arent, "Finding the Best Donors."

11. Wolfman-Arent, "Finding the Best Donors."

Chapter 4

1. Bruce Horovitz, "Big-Spending Baby Boomers Bend the Rules of Marketing," *USA Today,* November 16, 2010, http://usatoday30.usatoday.com/money/advertising/2010-11-16-1Aboomerbuyers16_CV_N.htm.

2. Robert Frank, "More Millionaires than Ever Are Living in the US," *CNBC,* March 10,2015, http://www.cnbc.com/2015/03/09/more-millionaires-than-ever-are-living-in-the-us.html.

3. Andy Kiersz, "Here's Where the Richest 10% Control the Bulk of a Country's Wealth," *Business Insider,* October 14, 2014, http://www.mybudget360.com/wealth-inequality-america-top-10-percent-of-us-households-control-75-percent-of-wealth/.

4. Paul G. Schervish, "America's Looming Philanthropic Revolution" *GenSpring Family Offices 2007 Family Symposium,* October 30, 2007, http://www.bc.edu/content/dam/files/research_sites/cwp/pdf/philanthropicrevolution.pdf.

5. Lynn Vavreck, "Definition of 'Rich' Changes with Income," *New York Times,* June 16, 2014, http://www.nytimes.com/2014/06/17/upshot/definition-of-rich-changes-with-income.html?_r=0&abt=0002&abg=1.

6. Steve Barkan, "Social Class in the United States," in *Sociology: Understanding and Changing the Social World,* accessed

June 25, 2015, http://www.peoi.org/Courses/Coursesen/socfwk/contents/frame8c.html.

7. Thomas J. Stanley and William D. Danko, *The Millionaire Next Door: The Surprising Secrets of American's Wealthy,* (New York: Long Street Press, 1996).

8. "Do You Fit the Profile That Wins More Sales?" *Salesforce,* 2014, https://www.salesforce.com/assets/pdf/misc/EB_Challenger.pdf.

Chapter 5

1. "Valuing Non-Cash Assets for Charity: What Donors Need to Know," *The Boston Foundation,* accessed June 23, 2015, http://www.tbf.org/tbf/65/complex-assets.

2. Les Christie, "America's Homes Are Bigger than Ever," *CNN Money,* June 5, 2014, http://money.cnn.com/2014/06/04/real_estate/american-home-size/.

3. John Egan, "U.S. Self-Storage Industry Statistics," *The Spare-Foot Storage Beat,* May 26, 2015, http://news.sparefoot.com/1432-self-storage-industry-statistics.

4. Joshua Becker, "21 Surprising Statistics That Reveal How Much Stuff We Actually Own," *Becoming Minimalist* (blog), accessed June 9, 2016, http://www.becomingminimalist.com/clutter-stats/.

5. Jura Koncius, "Stuff It: Millennials Nix Their Parents' Treasures," *The Washington Post,* March 27, 2015, https://www.washingtonpost.com/locaboomers-unwanted-inheritance/2015/03/27/0e75ff6e-45c4-11e4-b437-1a7368204804_story.html.

6. "Non-Cash Gifts Boosted Corporate Giving," *The NonProfit*

Times, January 3, 2011, http://www.thenonprofittimes.com/ news-articles/non-cash-gifts-boosted-corporate-giving/.

7. Michael Stroik, *Giving in Numbers: 2014 Edition*, The Committee Encouraging Corporate Philanthropy, accessed June 23, 2015, http://cecp.co/pdfs/giving_in_numbers/ GIN2014_Web_Final.pdf.

Chapter 6

1. Steven Lawry, "Is Charity Navigator About to Veer Off Course?" *Humanitarian & Development NGOs Domain* (blog), March 8, 2010, http://hausercenter.org/iha/2010/03/08/is-charity-navigator-about-to-veer-off-course/.

2. Dan Pallotta, *Charity Case: How the Nonprofit Community Can Stand Up for Itself and Really Change the World* (San Francisco: Jossey-Bass, 2012).

3. "Climbing Lessons: How Four Organizations Ascended the Philanthropy 400," *Chronicle of Philanthropy* 28, no. 1 (2015): 19.

Chapter 7

1. David Callahan, "Philanthropy Forecast, 2017: Trends and Issues to Watch," *Inside Philanthropy,* January 18, 2017, https://www.insidephilanthropy.com/home/2017/1/18/ philanthropy-forecast-2017.

2. "Taking Care of Business," *Chronicle of Philanthropy* 27, no. 11 (2015): 14.

3. "Innovative Finance," *The Rockefeller Foundation,* accessed June 23, 2015, http://www.rockefellerfoundation.org/our-work/initiatives/innovative-finance/.

4. Aimee Minnich, interview with the author, June 3, 2015.

5. Minnich.

6. "Capital Creation—A Divine Perspective," *Eventide*, July 29, 2015, http://eventidefunds.com/faith-and-business/capital-creation-a-divine-perspective/.

7. Bill High and Aimee Minnich, "Ministry Enterprise: Grow Revenue and Accelerate Impact" (presentation, Outcomes Conference of the Christian Leadership Alliance, Dallas, TX, April 2015).

Chapter 8

1. Simon Sinek, "Start with Why: How Great Leaders Inspire Action," TEDx Talks, uploaded September 28, 2009, https://www.youtube.com/watch?v=u4ZoJKF_VuA.

2. Carmine Gallo, *Talk Like Ted* (New York: St. Martin's Press, 2014), 72-73.

3. Chip Heath and Dan Heath, *Made to Stick: Why Some Ideas Survive and Others Die* (New York: Random House, 2008), 84-85.

4. Heath and Heath, *Made to Stick*, 226-230.

5. Rob Wu, "How to Get Started in Storytelling for Fundraising—Cara Jones Interview," *The CauseVox Blog*, accessed June 23, 2015, http://www.causevox.com/blog/how-to-get-started-in-storytelling-for-fundraising-cara-jones-interview/.

6. Heath and Heath, *Made to Stick*, 165-167.

7. "Statistics," *YouTube*, accessed July 28, 2015, https://www.youtube.com/yt/press/statistics.html.

Chapter 9

1. Joseph J. Thorndike, "How the Charity Deduction Made the World Safe for Philanthropy," *Tax Analysts,* December 13, 2012, http://www.taxhistory.org/thp/readings.nsf/Art-Web/972168BEA0B68D8585257B160048DD4A?OpenDocument.

2. Thorndike, "Charity Deduction".

3. Daniel J. Mitchell and Diana Aviv, "Should We End the Tax Deduction for Charitable Donations?" *Wall Street Journal,* December 16, 2012, http://www.wsj.com/articles/SB100014 24127887324469304578143351470610998.

4. Mitchell and Aviv, "Should We End."

5. Dan Busby, interview with author, June 4, 2015.

6. Jessica Levinsohn, "30% of Annual Charitable Donations Made in December" *New York Post,* December 21, 2013, http://nypost.com/2013/12/21/30-of-annual-charitable-donations-made-in-dec/.

7. Mike Patton, "US Debt Is Heading Toward $20 Trillion: Where It's Been, Where It's Going and Why," *Forbes,* March 28, 2016, http://www.forbes.com/sites/mikepatton/2016/03/28/u-s-debt-is-heading-toward-20-trillion-where-its-been-where-its-going-and-why/#5e5c86bb3a0c.

8. Patton, "US Debt."

9. David Longstreet, "Private Charity vs. Government Entitlements," working paper, accessed Sept. 16, 2016, http://www.softwaremetrics.com/Economics/Private%20Charity%20versus%20Government%20Entitlements.pdf.

10. Longstreet, "Private Charity."

11. Howard Husock, "Lesson for April 15: Why Government Can't Replace Charity," *Forbes*, April 10, 2014, http://www.forbes.com/sites/howardhusock/2014/04/10/lesson-for-april-15-why-government-cant-replace-charity/#1aee19841050.

12. Husock, "Lesson."

13. Busby, interview.

Chapter 10

1. "Best Jobs—Financial Advisor Overview," *US News & World Report*, accessed Sept. 9, 2016, http://money.usnews.com/careers/best-jobs/financial-advisor.

2. Robert Frank, "More Millionaires than Ever Are Living in the U.S." *CNBC*, March 10, 2015, http://www.cnbc.com/id/102489739.

3. Jerry Nuerge (owner, Financial Independence Group), interview with the author, June 9, 2015.

4. Lilly Family School of Philanthropy, "The 2014 U.S. Trust Study of High Net Worth Philanthropy," *Indiana University-Purdue University Indianapolis*, accessed June 26, 2015, http://www.philanthropy.iupui.edu/files/image/101614-philanthropystats-v11.pdf.

5. Sarah Lincoln and Joe Saxton, "Major Donor Giving Research Report: A Synthesis of the Current Research into Major Donors and Philanthropic Giving," *Institute of Fundraising*, July 2012, http://www.institute-of-fundraising.org.uk/library/major-donor-giving-research-report/.

6. Michael King (vice president, Gift Planning Services, National Christian Foundation), interview with the author, June 19, 2015.

7. *2015 Giving Report, Fidelity Charitable,* accessed August 10, 2015, http://www.fidelitycharitable.org/giving-report/.

8. Ron Blue (president, Kingdom Advisors), interview with the author, June 10, 2015.

9. Marty Bicknell, interview with the author, August 17, 2016.

10. "Growth in Recent Years," *National Philanthropic Trust,* accessed October 13, 2016, https://www.nptrust.org/daf-report/recent-growth.html.

Chapter 11

1. Christian Smith and Hilary Davidson, *The Paradox of Generosity: Giving We Receive, Grasping We Lose* (New York: Oxford UP, 2014), 4.

2. Christian Smith and Hilary Davidson, *Paradox*, 26-27.

3. Eric Foley, *Coach Your Champions: The Transformational Giving Approach to Major Donor Fundraising* (Colorado Springs: Mission Increase Foundation, 2009).

4. Prov. 11:25, New International Version.

5. Smith and Davidson, *Paradox*, 56-59.

6. Smith and Davidson, *Paradox*, 78-79.

7. Smith and Davidson, *Paradox*, 63-70.

8. William F. High, *The Generosity Bet* (Shippensburg, PA: Destiny Image, 2014), 137.

9. Rick Warren with Tom Holladay, "Teaching Your People to Be Generous," *Generous Giving*, accessed June 23, 2015, http://library.generousgiving.org/articles/display.asp?id=181.

10. Smith and Davidson, *Paradox*, 99-100.

ABOUT THE AUTHORS

Bill High is CEO and general counsel for The Signatry, a Global Christian Foundation in suburban Kansas City. Before starting the foundation, as a graduate of the University of Kansas School of Law, High was a partner in a major Kansas City law firm and currently remains of counsel for another firm. He lives in Lenexa, Kansas, with his wife, Brooke, and has four children.

Ray Gary has been starting and growing businesses for nearly thirty years. He is currently the CEO of iDonate. Before taking over iDonate, he was CEO at Cleverspring, an e-learning company. He was also president at Koch Ventures, a marketing and advertising company. He holds a bachelor's degree in business administration from the University of Oklahoma, and he currently resides in Dallas, Texas.

Made in the USA
Lexington, KY
13 April 2018